ERIN BROCKOVICH
AND THE
BEVERLY HILLS
GREENSCAM

ERIN BROCKOVICH
AND THE
BEVERLY HILLS
GREENSCAM

NORMA ZAGER

PELICAN PUBLISHING COMPANY
GRETNA 2010

The word *"Pelican"* and the depiction of a pelican are
trademarks of Pelican Publishing Company, Inc., and are
registered in the U.S. Patent and Trademark Office.

Library of Congress Cataloging-in-Publication Data

Zager, Norma.
  Erin Brockovich and the Beverly Hills greenscam / Norma
Zager.
    p. cm.
  ISBN 978-1-58980-810-2 (hardcover : alk. paper)
  1. Brockovich, Erin. 2. Environmentalists—United States. 3.
Environmental ethics. 4. Beverly Hills High School (Beverly
Hills, Calif.)—Trials, litigation, etc. 5. Liability for hazardous
substances pollution damages—California. 6. Beverly Hills
(Calif.)—Environmental conditions. I. Title.
  GE56.B76Z34 2010
  363.70092—dc22

                                        2010029042

Printed in the United States of America
Published by Pelican Publishing Company, Inc.
1000 Burmaster Street, Gretna, Louisiana 70053

*Dedicated with love to my children,
my parents, and my grandson.*

Contents

Acknowledgments

Special thanks and hugs to Barry Brucker, Mark Egerman, Jody Kleinman, and Ari Bussel for all their help and for allowing me to constantly test their memories. Their input throughout the entire seven years of the case was invaluable and greatly appreciated. I am sending them a big "thank-you" for sticking it out with me until the end. Each made the tough questions easier to answer; the sad, frustrating moments easier to endure; and the entire process all the more pleasant by their company.

Thank you to Harry Waterstone, who was the backbone of the editorial department. His support was immeasurable.

A special thank-you to *Courier* publisher March Schwartz. When he hired me he said it was because he believed I could handle anything that came along. Fortuitous words indeed.

Thanks to all those in the city, schools, and Air Quality Management District and to Mark Katchen for helping gather information, answering my emails and phone calls, and offering facts and opinions with the sole intent of truthful journalism. I appreciate every one of you, and your input was incalculable. To my friends who propped me up and offered a shoulder to lean on through the best and worst of times, you all deserve accolades.

A thank-you to Danny for the great education on "big oil,"

Dr. Wendy Cozen for her patience and generous sharing of her expertise, Mark Scott for his honesty, Dr. Gwen Gross for believing, and Sam Atwood for his frequent contributions to a burgeoning environmental conscience.

To Larry Wiener and Janice, Laura, and Byron Pope for all their help and information gathering and to Roey Urman for his input.

Thank-you to my editor Lindsey Reynolds, a breath of fresh air in a sea of VOCs.

A special thank-you to Fred Hayman, who established the "Beverly Hills Standard" and constantly reminds me of my responsibility to achieve those lofty levels.

1

Tarnished Tinsel

Strip away the phony tinsel of Hollywood and you'll find the real tinsel underneath.

—Oscar Levant

The subject was cancer; the issue, controversy over the effectiveness of a city's oversight of an oil well on their high-school campus. Allegations of sickness and death and a community's fears are about to be discussed on a news program reaching millions of viewers. The guest is introduced and the interviewer, an attorney-turned-talk-show-host, smiles broadly with anticipation. The audience gears up for a barrage of hard-hitting questions aimed at this proponent of environmental responsibility and champion for the victims.

The attorney-host leans in intently, stares his subject in the face, and prepares to unleash a firestorm of focused and relevant questions concerning the guest's latest battle against evil corporate polluters. The subject's smile is welcoming and ingenuous, her hair pulled back in a ponytail, donning a turtleneck sweater and a vest. She is a picture of all things Ozzie and Harriet, America's sweetheart, the country's own little "green" darling.

The host speaks, each word carefully and thoughtfully designed to elicit the desired response. Years of courtroom experience have molded him into a master at honing in on the heart of the matter, revealing all to a rapt jury. His first question must speak to the seriousness of the allegations, the cancers, the blatant and egregious pollution violations, and the suffering of children. His mouth opens to unleash an opening salvo as the audience holds its collective breath. But as he leans closer, his demeanor suddenly shifts to that of a high-school boy asking for a prom date. He asks with all seriousness, "So, what's it like to be Erin Brockovich?"

Perhaps the more appropriate question would have been, "Who is Erin Brockovich?" Most know Erin as a miniskirted, cleavaged mistress of doom who would harm the innocent. In the movie starring Julia Roberts about her lawsuit against Pacific Gas and Electric in Hinckley, California, we were introduced to someone with enormous compassion, inner strength, and no qualms about using her feminine advantages for good. In the movie about her life, Albert Finney's character questions how she will extract necessary evidence. Julia Roberts cups and elevates her breasts and says, "They're called boobs, Ed."

This is the Erin of legend, the one with whom most are acquainted as the hero for a new "green" consciousness. Perhaps it is ironic that a glimpse of another Erin should come in the very city that created and guards that image. But when the tinsel tarnished and the stage went dark, was there a far different character left on the stage than the one we had come to know? It has become extremely difficult to detach the real Erin from her movie character. Her name is now synonymous with those who would selflessly fight for all things green and good. Years of effective promotion by a highly skilled Beverly

Hills public relations team has sealed her image as an iron butterfly, forceful enough to battle the enemy but feminine enough to be embraced in our heart of hearts. A perfect pitch, even perhaps the perfect disguise.

Yet, following her foray into the glam capital of the world, Beverly Hills, I, as so many others, was left to ponder the identity of the real Erin Brockovich. Is she the cherry on Al Gore's toxic sundae? Or perhaps a highly effective "greenscam" artist, who like most celebrities disappoint when confronted on a personal level, when they step off the big screen and rejoin us mere mortals. The Erin Brockovich her handlers market publically ultimately proved a far cry from the one who entered Beverly Hills in full battle regalia.

It was a fight that proved to be an even match in most respects as the two sides called up their troops. Erin, a picture of innocence, yet savvy, successful, and comfortably settled into her new, wealthy lifestyle, was a feminine warrior with the acumen of a Sun Tzu marching into battle with a team of fully funded corporate lawyers. On the opposite side of the field, Beverly Hills, long the poster child for excess and extravagance, a city with legendary deep pockets and an aversion to payouts that would leave the city a little poorer and their adversaries a great deal richer. Who would battle more fiercely? Those who fought to secure newfound treasure or those for whom treasure was an inherited possession?

Erin's flawlessly crafted script was rife with effective methods guaranteed to achieve a desired result, one that would leave Erin and her partners with more green in their wallets and the city with far less. The story of the Beverly Hills oil well didn't follow the usual pattern, but instead in true Hollywood fashion delivered a surprise ending. Perhaps in chronicling these events the question of who is the "real" Erin will ultimately be revealed.

The Erin Brockovich Beverly Hills story began after dark on November 3, 2002, when Erin illegally trespassed on the campus of Beverly Hills High School (BHHS) and collected air samples she later described to me as "higher than the 405 Freeway at rush hour."

Former Beverly Hills High School student and Hodgkin's lymphoma victim Lori Moss contacted Erin after Moss met fellow student and Hodgkin's patient Dana Goodman during a doctor's visit. They quickly discovered they weren't the only BHHS students stricken with or dying from cancer. Later diagnosed with thyroid cancer, Moss grew more suspicious about what she believed to be an excessive number of cancers in fellow classmates. This suspicion in concert with a disturbing number of cancers occurring in younger adults and in multiples fueled her concerns.

News of a potential cancer cluster caught Erin and partner Ed Masry's attention, leading them on a stealth mission to collect data for an extensive court battle. Brockovich's sampling and subsequent results were unknown to city or school officials until months later on February 4, 2003, when disclosed during sweeps week on the Los Angeles CBS affiliate.

Why Erin withheld test results concerning substances potentially harmful to children until months later and chose to expose them under the guise of a sweeps week news story is a question that remains unanswered—except when examined in the context of the "sex sells" theory of the green world. High-profile media exposure is how most communities learn about Erin's visits. Possible problems at the high school, in themselves not so exciting, coupled with the "Green Queen" equals big ratings for networks.

On January 9, 2007, Superior Court judge Wendell Mortimer granted a summary judgment motion from the

City of Beverly Hills, releasing them from liability in the over 900 lawsuits filed regarding the oil wells. Legally, the city was almost off the hook, but the battle continued to rage as legal hours tallied to astronomical heights.

The years between the events were filled with tests, legal posturing, and indictments, temporarily igniting a rebirth of environmental awareness in a city whose high-profile reputation remains a consummate symbol of materialism. In reality, however, this story began long before the lawsuit. More than thirty years earlier the city of Beverly Hills entered into a contract with Beverly Hills Oil Company and gave the nod to the responsible government agencies. And that may very well be when the benzene hit the fan.

Beverly Hills residents had long been aware of the pungent odors blanketing the athletic fields at the high school. Students and parents running the track, playing baseball, and sitting in the bleachers observing had from time to time noted unpleasant smells offending their senses. When many complained about the well's existence, explanations were offered and accepted.

Was there any validity to the claims illnesses were a result of the well's proximity to the school and can anyone be certain of the conclusions based on what is currently known and accepted in the scientific community? Who should be blamed? Did emissions bear any responsibility for illness? The city assumed the agencies were responsible, parents assumed the city was on top of things, and while everyone was assuming, were the polluters having a heyday?

The awareness peaked in 1999 when Beverly Hills was first introduced to real environmental issues. Parents, not tort lawyers, led the charge at that time against the health problems and approached the school board, where Barry

Brucker was serving as president. Ironically, Brucker was also president when Erin Brockovich entered the Beverly Hills scene four years later.

I received a phone call from Barry around nine o'clock the evening the story was to be aired. Since I was the media point person in Beverly Hills, these calls were not uncommon. Caught off guard and excited by the deluge of requests for interviews from reporters, Barry sought an appropriate response. "No comment": that had to be the mantra until they found out what was really occurring at the well and what the allegations implied. To the credit of school district superintendent Dr. Gwen Gross, the city council, and school board, they acted quickly and ultimately kept the lid on what could have become a pot boiling over with greater fear and suspicion than Erin Brockovich and Ed Masry managed to cook up in their well-equipped kitchen.

2

The Appearance of Truth

To you everything that's happening in the world appears phony, to be something other than what it really is, right?
—J. D. Salinger

Following the initial CBS report alleging dangerous conditions at the high school, the district and city moved swiftly to ensure the safety of the children, staff, and faculty. The next few weeks brought a flurry of testing, statements of support, and meetings. A cache of scientists, government agencies, doctors, experts, and terrified parents melded into the city's glamorous landscape. Words like benzene, hexavalent chromium, and toluene replaced Prada, Gucci, and Tiffany in residents' vocabularies.

Beverly Hills Unified School District superintendent Dr. Gwen Gross and school board president Barry Brucker immediately ordered an investigation into irregularities and possible health hazards by Venoco, Inc., operator of the facility located at the high school. Venoco had already ceased operations at the site until air samples could be collected and analyzed by the Air Quality Management District (AQMD) and resolve a coincidental notice of violation for illegal venting of natural gas. This violation could not have come at a worse time to a community rife with allegations about supposed environmental issues.

Automated phone calls were made to notify parents of students at the high school. Dr. Gross opened the next school board meeting with a statement clarifying the situation and reassuring everyone that steps were being taken to investigate well safety. In her statement she explained to parents, "A local reporter told us on February 4 that a law firm was making allegations about the air quality at the high school. We instantly enlisted the assistance of our expert, Mark Katchen, who, in coordination with the AQMD and using state-of-the-art techniques, sampled the ambient air on campus the following Thursday morning. On both Friday and Saturday mornings, further AQMD tests were also conducted."

AQMD spokesman Sam Atwood issued a statement at the conclusion of testing: "We were extremely pleased to learn that the results demonstrated no abnormal conditions and were consistent with other monitoring stations operated by the California Air Resources Board. In addition, today we received assurances from Venoco that it will 'voluntarily remain shut down to allow background air sampling.'" Rod Eson, then president and CEO of Venoco Inc., sent a letter to the school district promising Venoco would only return to production in consultation with the AQMD.

Barry Wallerstein, AQMD executive officer and BHHS graduate, informed the city, "Specifically during the morning hours, a twenty-minute sample had been taken on the athletic field with sub-samples taken at the beginning and end of the overall sampling period. In addition, three instantaneous grab samples were taken that evening at the ball field, Shirley Place, and Moreno Drive. The AQMD also sampled the well gas directly at the vent pipe during the evening sample process. Well gas was being vented by the facility at the top of the oil rig during the morning and evening sampling."

According to Atwood, two separate samplings were done from the bleachers near the ball field. One was sent to the Columbia Analytical Services laboratories in Simi Valley; the other was analyzed at the AQMD laboratory in Diamond Bar. The results of those tests were in compliance with the testing stations for the Los Angeles Basin, located in Burbank and the City of Commerce, and "far lower than the Masry law firm's reported findings."

In a conversation with Michael Tuday, director of Research and Development at Columbia Analytical Services in Simi Valley, who tested samplings from both the law firm and the AQMD, I was told, "When you're sampling you don't want to base health-risk decisions on a single sample result—that would be irresponsible."

Despite reassurances, many parents were unsatisfied with the results, claiming they were taken when the wells were not operational. Beverly Hills High School alumni Ari Bussel is among those who questioned the legitimacy of any comparisons: "For the better part of two decades in the eighties and nineties, the oil company acted with no supervision. They vented whatever they needed into the atmosphere, right over the high school, walled on one side by the high-rise towers of Century City. Is it surprising that students and teachers could smell and sometimes see the volatile organic compounds?"

Bussel was not surprised Venoco was cooperating. "These were very rich oil wells. A multitude of drillings, both of oil and natural gas, and now, when a notice of violation for illegal venting is issued, the corporate-responsible culprit that throughout the decades did exactly what it wanted to do is behaving."

Jim Drury, an environmental specialist employed by the Masry & Vititoe law firm, conducted the tests for Brockovich. According to Drury, he performed an eight-hour sampling with a stainless-steel Summa canister. "These containers are sterilized to eliminate any previous residue," Drury said. "We have a slow intake valve to accumulate air samples over a long period." Drury claimed his samples were considerably higher in toxins than those taken by AQMD. I asked about the sampling procedures and the obvious discrepancies in the data. He responded, "Everyone has to go on faith that we collected these samples at the playing field next to Venoco. Chains of custody, mappings, and the rest are not really important. What's important are the results found by an internationally recognized air lab."

It was the "go on faith" part the city was having trouble accepting. A subsequent meeting between the district and Masry's law firm failed to yield the specific information about Drury's tests the school's representatives were hoping to glean. The unanswered questions surrounding locations and protocol created suspicion regarding Masry's actual results. "We aren't releasing any of that information," Drury said. "This is a preliminary investigation and you can believe me when I say they were taken at the high-school field." When asked if the source may be other than the school field, he said they were just beginning to investigate and would look at other potential pollutant causes in the area. "We have experience in evaluating these toxic pollutants and we will leave no stone unturned."

What the original meeting did glean, however, was an insight into the next few years. Claims and allegations flowed freely, many times without sufficient evidence or support. The city was being asked to "trust" that the tests and methods of Brockovich and her team were truthful and revealed legitimate dangers to the health of the community, past and present. Many had no trouble doing exactly that, but others were not quite so anxious to jump on board the tort law train.

Dr. Gross recalls Ed Masry's invitation to meet at his office. "We were suspicious of Masry's motives at the outset. Our attorney, Dave Orbach, advised me not to see him because they could have been baiting me. We were afraid there would be news cameras, so I let Dave go, but Masry was angry I'd sent a lawyer. He's a lawyer, so why would he be so surprised to see Dave?"

The district's environmental expert, Mark Katchen, who attended that meeting, called it "very bizarre." He describes, "We went expecting Masry to show us his data, but he kept stonewalling us and wanted ours. His risk assessment people were there and that was really strange. They kept saying they could help us and it seemed like they were trying to solicit business from the schools."

Although the city seemed to be handling it all well, behind the scenes it was a different matter. Dr. Gross remembers her initial contact with the CBS producer Claudia de la Pena and says she still retains distaste for the station's methods and behavior. "Coincidently, there was some mold discovered that day on tiles at Hawthorne Elementary as a result of modernization. Claudia de la Pena called and told me she had heard through 'some attorney in the valley' there was an environmental problem at the school. She asked if I would come and speak to the attorney when she found out what law firm that was. I was surprised she was asking me about a lawyer.

"Later, I received a call from Ed Masry asking me to meet with him to resolve the issue. I still wasn't even sure what the issue was all about.

"I thought to myself at the time, this is odd. How would she know about the mold from some attorney?"

According to Dr. Gross, local CBS reporter Drew Griffin, now with news channel CNN, seemed unusually aggressive with her. She recalls her upset when he tricked her and staged an interview to which she never agreed. "He asked me if I would answer his questions and I said no. He didn't tell me he had a microphone in his pocket and was taping me. Then he showed a picture of me on the newscast and used the tape as though I had answered. I was so angry, there was my picture they'd downloaded from the website and comments I didn't even know he was recording onto a microphone hidden in his pocket, and it made it look like he'd interviewed me.

"CBS News and Drew Griffin were not news broadcasters; they were newsmakers. Had it not been the hocus-pocus fabrication of a cancer exposure at Beverly Hills High School, CBS probably would have run a story about Martians landing on Santa Monica beach.

"If I remember correctly, I must have said, 'I am not familiar with any dangerous cancer-causing element at the oil well next door, but we take very seriously the health and welfare of our students and staff.' I also mentioned that this was the first I had heard about any problems at our high school."

After the story aired, an interesting fact came to light. The new information led to serious questions of bias in the minds of many school officials. According to Dr. Gross, public information shared with the board connoted that there was a personal relationship between local KCBS producer Claudia de la Pena and the Masry law firm. Records showed Ed Masry and de la Pena both served as members of the Thousand Oaks City Council. California campaign form 260 for de la Pena disclosed evidence that Ed and Joette Masry contributed financially to de la Pena's campaign.

When I called de la Pena to verify the story, she denied having anything but a professional relationship with Masry. "I don't think that ethically speaking the two should be mixed together," de la Pena insisted. "Even though I produced the story, the majority was handled by the reporter. If you are looking at a connection between the city council and my producing, it is not the right route to go from a journalistic standpoint. You have to be able to absolutely separate the two." She refused to comment further and I ran the story, eliciting a harsh and insulting e-mail from Drew Griffin, her reporter.

"It is obvious there is far more to this story than mere coincidence," Brucker commented at the time.

Even with the questions surrounding the Masry/de la Pena relationship, Dr. Gross admits that during the initial weeks, she began to have fears about the truth of the allegations. "You start to worry, 'Oh my God, could this be true?' But I realized that it was nothing when Dr. Wendy Cozen, a noted epidemiologist, reassured me about the science and cancer types and numbers. With her and our own environmental expert, Mark Katchen, disputing the claims, I finally relaxed."

She remembers her initial response to the appearance of a truck parked outside the school with a banner reading, "If you know anyone who has cancer sign up here." She relates, "I knew we were in trouble when I saw what looked like an ice-cream truck parked right outside the high school, not far from our office, recruiting people. They were there day in and day out for weeks."

School board member Alissa Roston recalls her strong reaction to the allegations: "I not only had two sons there, but both my boys were on the soccer team. They were running in that dirt every day and I wanted to know whether or not it was safe." Roston says she couldn't recall whether or not there were any discussions about closing the school, but closing the soccer field was considered right away. She says there was a real sense of urgency about completing the testing as quickly as possible.

In the midst of all the testing and verifying normal levels of toxic chemicals in ambient air samples, Masry maintained the campus was dangerous. When asked if he felt the school was harmful, Masry replied he would have no trouble sending his child to Beverly Hills High School as long as "that well wasn't operating."

Brucker verifies there was never any intention to close the school: "There was never a discussion about closing the school. The mere fact Erin Brockovich and Ed Masry had done their testing months earlier and never informed us about any health concerns made us very suspicious. The only conversation the school board had was about removing kids from the playfield on the south side of the campus, adjacent to the oil well.

"In addition, we were in touch from day one with Mark Katchen to assess exposure risks. Unlike the plaintiffs' junk science evaluations and non-verifiable testing methods, the city and the school district embarked upon a methodical and scientifically sound testing protocol.

"From the start comments were made about another movie deal. In the February 2003 issue of *Variety,* Masry and Brockovich commented about potential movie rights. It was obvious they were excited at the prospects of such a high-profile target."

Brucker says they were aware "from the first moment" that there were huge flaws in their story. "Sweeps week, junk science testing protocols, exposure levels that were outrageously misleading were all part of the shock broadcasting tactics employed by CBS in Los Angeles. Interestingly, the other networks didn't cover the events, for they too were suspicious of the quality of the story and the credibility of the science."

Following the initial shock at Erin's foray onto the BHHS campus, the attorneys' tasks began in earnest. Securing plaintiffs was a crucial part of the Masry team's strategy. It was soon apparent that the lawyer's time-tested methods were about to open the floodgates and unleash a legal tidal wave to inundate Beverly Hills.

Shortly after the news stories and accusations died down a bit, the city was invited to a greenscam gala at a familiar haunt and treated to a healthy menu of Chicken Little rhetoric. Served up on a well-worn platter of scare tactics, that first client-recruiting meeting was as finely honed as the one-liners in a Neil Simon comedy, and at times equally amusing. Had not the subject been so morbid and tragic, more laughs may have been forthcoming. Yet it was an effective means to an end and numerous plaintiffs were enlisted following the evening's festivities.

Tempers flared and fears escalated that evening as Ed Masry and Erin Brockovich spoke before the overflowing crowd of more than five hundred in the packed Crystal Ballroom of the opulent Beverly Hills Hotel. The room's plush carpet was hidden under rows of chairs in lieu of elegantly appointed tables sporting lush, designer floral arrangements and linen napkins. Couture gowns and Jimmy Choo shoes were conspicuously absent. Instead seats were filled with angry, worried parents eager and determined to discover more about a dangerous health threat to their community than hobnob with the Beverly Hills glitterati. As the local reporter on scene, I was resolved to pay close attention to the arguments on both sides. I had already gathered a great deal of information and was fully ready to disregard any celebrity hype and put my faith in the science.

I can attest to the fact that there was no party atmosphere in that elegant ballroom that evening. The chic surroundings were overshadowed by fears of cancer clusters, poisons spewing through the air, and harmful chemicals. The firm alleged the well was the cause for what they termed "frighteningly high numbers of cancers in Beverly Hills High School alumni," covering the years from 1975 to 1997 and approximately eleven thousand graduates.

Choreographed to meet even the standards of one of Beverly Hills' most illustrious residents, Gene Kelly, the backdrop was a massive, almost ceiling height, picture of the flower-strewn well, looming menacingly above the crowd. The ominous image framed Erin as she stood, professional in a dark business suit, dwarfed before the well's image. No sexy miniskirts and cleavage for the audience that evening. She was deep into her role of serious environmental crusader and determined to live up to her role as America's Green Queen.

Brockovich began the evening by issuing a disclaimer about her intentions: "This is not a publicity stunt, there is no movie being sold here." She explained that when she began the case she knew she would be in for harsh criticism when dealing with a high-profile city like Beverly Hills. Resident reaction to Erin's presence varied. Some were impressed by her fame; others, suspicious of motives. There were of course the true believers who feared she had once again found a pot of black gold in Beverly Hills' rainbow—perhaps even at the expense of their children's health.

Ed Masry, crusty and as curmudgeon-like as Spencer Tracy portraying Clarence Darrow, cited 170 confirmed cancer cases, 147 of which were Beverly Hills High alumni (approximately half men and half women). A slide show presented facts and figures about noxious gases like benzene, hexane, and other volatile organic compounds with which most residents, including me, had had little or merely a nodding acquaintance until that February.

The meeting was quite antagonistic as though sides had already been chosen. The undecided were being coerced to "get in line." Benign questions were shouted down or disregarded angrily by the Masry team. When parent Jody Kleinman asked if they would be willing to share test results, she was rudely interrupted and dismissed by Masry, who claimed that he had offered to share all testing and would comment no further. Objectivity was in short supply and accusations flowed like the very oil they were vilifying. I was convinced by the end of the evening that this legal approach was a scripted and rehearsed program initiated to guarantee recruits.

Masry asked those who chose to stay for the second part of the meeting to fill out a health questionnaire and informed them about lawsuits the firm would be pursuing. Apparently, there would be a class-action suit for those who were injured directly and a medical monitoring suit for all BHHS graduates. Perhaps a third of the room remained for the second half of the meeting. When those not interested in the lawsuit were asked to leave, I left. Those who stayed received a folder containing a questionnaire, letters, and law firm information. I believe they were asked to sign their names to a list before receiving these packets.

Interestingly, this list may have been used for more than informational purposes. Two of the plaintiffs in the suit were unaware of their involvement until I informed them that their names were among the plaintiff forms I had received. I speculated it was the result of signing the list at the informational meeting. Those two plaintiffs remained in the case, choosing to follow it through to a natural conclusion.

During the course of the meeting, many charges were leveled that I believed would be unfair to leave unanswered in my subsequent article covering the event. Brockovich and

Masry both claimed the Air Quality Management District had been uncooperative when contacted early on. When reached the next day, AQMD director Dr. Barry Wallerstein, a BHHS grad, disputed these claims. "I have been calling back individual parents since this started. Why wouldn't I call back Masry? The only call we received aside from interested parents was from [local station] KCBS."

According to Wallerstein, all air test results thus far had been within normal ranges. "We did grab samples before and eight-hour sampling when the well went back on and we will be doing more samples once the oil well is fully operational." He was adamant, "We have found nothing to independently confirm the sampling reported by Masry."

Wallerstein addressed an issue Erin raised concerning abandoned wells: "Abandoned fields would come under our testing sampling. We took samples in the middle of the field and the bleachers as well."

During the course of the informational meeting, Masry had accused the school district of not doing their job to protect the children and claimed their negligence had led to the alleged high rate of cancers and illnesses in former as well as current students. School district environmentalist Mark Katchen of the Phylmar Group answered Masry's claims. He noted that although the numbers are disturbing, there is a process that must be followed to establish whether or not the numbers extend beyond the norm. "Control groups must be set up and the proper process followed before anyone can say for sure whether these numbers are indeed high."

Masry's claim that the district had failed to test air samples was also disputed by Katchen, who said indoor air quality sampling was done in 1999 and the results were perfectly within normal ranges. He noted that any elevated levels of chemicals in the air had existed only temporarily over the years. "Whenever we found any issue of a concentration of a chemical that was slightly elevated, it was due to a transient maintenance operation like a repair of a wall panel using a glue that contained a solvent, for example. Once that was repaired it quickly dissipated and dropped down to safe levels."

Responding to Masry's allegations that noxious odors had been prevalent at the well site and should have been addressed, Katchen stressed that one's sense of smell picks up odors at levels so low they do not have a health impact, so smell is not always a good indicator of a health risk. "The smell might cause you to be uncomfortable, but not necessarily at risk," he explained.

However, Masry was adamant his samples could hold up in any court and he would ultimately prove his claims. "I know we know what we know, and our test results showed what they showed. We are willing to debate anyone and we are not hiding anything." Brockovich, Masry, and their experts pointed the finger at the AQMD, the City of Beverly Hills, and its school district for ignoring the potential danger. Masry alleged they covered up the situation and allowed the attorneys to discount health issues. "They are only concerned about money. They are trying to protect their financial interests," Masry barked angrily at the meeting.

Beverly Hills Municipal League president and meeting attendee Thomas White demanded Masry state whether or not he intended to sue the city and school district. "In the beginning I was willing to work with them," Masry answered. "But they broke appointments, stood us up at meetings, and refused to split samples with us, so now we will do what we must." He informed attendees that under the laws of the state there exists a six-month window in which a suit can be filed, and he fully intended to meet the six-month statute of limitations.

Beverly Hills School Board president Barry Brucker later disputed Masry's allegations that they had refused to sample. He insisted the city and schools were not disputing the cancers exist, but only whether or not they were above normal levels and if in fact the source was environmental. "Mark Katchen took tests, as well as the AQMD, and they all came back within the normal ranges," Brucker stated after the meeting. "That's what we've been saying all along. No one other than Masry has shown numbers that put the emissions outside of any normal range."

When questioned on the perception of their lack of responsiveness, Brucker insisted that at that point the community knew whatever the board knew. "We will continue to acquire data until we are satisfied we have all the information. Our policy is if there is nothing to hide, hide nothing."

As the evening at the Beverly Hills Hotel drew to a close, many of the BHHS graduates who had attended left with more questions concerning the dangers. There was also a determination by residents and teachers to uncover the validity of Brockovich's claims.

Following the meeting, I spoke with former student Lisa Lewis, a thyroid cancer survivor and 1996 Beverly Hills High graduate. She was one of the first contacted by the trial lawyers when the case began but stated she was not a participant in the lawsuit. Lewis told me she doubted claims the cancers resulted from attending the school. "I don't feel they have proven sufficiently [that] the school or city is to blame. I have inquired on my own and my doctors have always said they don't think the [cancer] numbers are abnormal.

"I loved my experience at Beverly Hills High and I wouldn't

have traded it for anything in the world. If there is a problem, then they should prove it or make sure they are out there testing every week to ensure it's safe. I had cancer five years ago and the past is the past. I want to make sure from here on in no one will be affected."

Lewis spoke emotionally about her reaction to the evening. "I came out of the meeting with negative feelings and when I left I cried hysterically for a half-hour. Everyone was yelling and unwilling to listen and it was a very negative environment. People were riled up and they were there with serious concerns, but their questions never got answered." Her anguish over the truth of the allegations was shared by many in the community.

However, not everyone was as benevolent toward the city or the school board. One resident, who declined to be named, was noticeably angry. "It's not enough to say we care about our children. Who doesn't care about their children? What I want to know is what are we doing about it? We should have our own expert out there every day if need be, and I don't care what it costs. Then we'll have our own numbers, not from the AQMD or Masry, who is building a lawsuit, but from someone just looking out for our interests."

One meeting participant, engineer and attorney Faryan Andrew Afifi, thanked and blessed Masry publicly for bringing the oil well's existence to the forefront. "Up until a month ago I didn't even know there was an oil well there," Afifi told the crowd. "I am going to stop that oil well from operating and I need your help. I need the data; will you give it to me?" Masry replied there was no problem sharing his data since he had already shared it with the press.

Longtime resident Jonathon Zimbert, a parent of a high-school student, was very unhappy with what he heard at the meeting. "My impression was that if they were flat-out wrong by half, it's still incredibly alarming. There's no denying the numbers are beyond coincidence." Zimbert believed there was a lack of determination on the city's behalf to get to the truth. "Strikes me as if there is more lip service than genuine action. The well is working again, but a couple weeks of it not working will not change anything. It will give some people at least some level of solace. This situation is being lawyered and that shouldn't be the number one priority."

Brockovich and Masry said the city could legally shut down the oil well if a health hazard exists and strongly suggested it be done. I broached the subject of closing the well with Venoco vice president Mike Edwards. He said the well would be shut down if there was a health hazard, but thus far no testing except Masry's had recorded any numbers out of the norm. "Most government entities have the ability to abate a health risk," Edwards explained. "For the general safety of the public one would hope the regulatory agency has the authority. We rely on the AQMD and if they identified an abnormality, we would do what was required. The AQMD monitors hundreds of gas and oil production sites throughout the L.A. Basin."

In response to the barrage of allegations and fears within the community before and after the Brockovich/Masry meeting, Dr. Gross sent the following memo to her staff to notify them of steps being taken to address their concerns.

> In response to faculty and staff concerns regarding indoor air quality, the District has retained Mark Katchen, Environmental Consultant from the Phylmar Group, to begin an assessment.
>
> To begin his assessment, he will be conducting 20-minute interviews with individuals who wish to provide him with input regarding their concerns.

If you sign up for an interview, it is important that you arrive promptly so that everyone will have an ample opportunity to discuss their concerns with Mr. Katchen.

The day following Erin's presentation I was notified a walkout had been scheduled for the next week at BHHS. Stephanie Pofcher, a 1994 Beverly graduate, was organizing the event for parents and students intent on making a larger statement about their concerns. "Our goal is to acquire our own environmental expert who would conduct independent testing in order to ease the stress and anxiety students and parents are feeling. There is a fear factor involved now. I have an autoimmune disease that does not run in my family and am in remission. The real concern for parents is if we should take our students out of school and what we need to do to make us feel more comfortable about sending our kids to Beverly Hills High."

Many concerned parents I spoke with in the days following the Brockovich meeting wanted more test results immediately. Yar Meshkaty, a civic leader and community activist, and his wife, Nooshin, who went on to later serve as school board president, attended the meeting to gather information. Yar had a different take on shutting down the wells immediately: "We are all worried; after all, we have our kids there. I don't think they should shut down the wells. If they do, how can we test to find out if the wells were the real culprit here?"

When I spoke to Wallerstein about Yar's concern, he responded, "I intend to issue a report within a couple of weeks summarizing our findings and providing comparisons to other locations, including other school sites. We just ask that the parents give us the appropriate time to do good science."

As time progressed, the definition of "good science"

became increasingly difficult to distinguish as "good tort law" entered the fray. And so came the Erin Brockovich/Ed Masry dog and pony show, focusing on a golden opportunity to enhance their reputations and collect copious amounts of money under the guise of exposing a dangerous health hazard. And they ran with the opportunity like Seabiscuit nearing the finish line.

But when the dust settled and the race was run, what really happened? What really went on beneath the high-profile rhetoric and publicity-crazed accusers? Was the result ultimately a price paid with doubt, fear, and a lasting scar on the city's oft-lifted appearance? Was it merely another attempt to make an end run around the legal system? An effort to create a well-heeled cash cow and line the pockets of individuals seizing an opportunity at the expense of a community and its residents? Interlaced in this drama lie varying degrees of pathos, humor, and a cache of knowledge waiting to be gleaned from the experience. A quiet undercurrent of fear drifted like a subtle breeze throughout the city, brought by a story fraught with emotion and ego, struggles between the greater good and smaller egocentric needs. For this is after all Beverly Hills, where power is paramount and manipulation practiced like piano scales by a concert pianist. In the end the players in this human drama created the dialogue. On a stage fraught with the creative elements guaranteed to entice and captivate any audience was a cast that could excel in a Pulitzer-caliber play. And lucky me, as the *Courier* reporter covering this story, I had a backstage, all-access pass.

3

A Flower-Bedecked Target

There is no dilemma compared with that of the deep-sea diver who hears the message from the ship above, "Come up at once. We are sinking."

—Robert Cooper

Much has been written and spoken about the infamous oil derrick on the high-school campus. Erin alluded to its secretive nature in interviews and claimed the flowered pattern covering the tower was designed to mask its presence. Titled Project 9865 and renamed the Tower of Hope, it was dedicated at a public ceremony on the athletic field. The tower features artwork panels done by chronically ill children throughout the state. Today, years later, it has become a shabby shadow of its former colorful exterior. Portions of the original panels hang off the derrick, torn and faded like the dead rising in Michael Jackson's "Thriller" video. Queries about when the panels will be removed and replaced are stonewalled by both the city and the oil company.

The series of art panels were originally part of a nonprofit project conceived by Ed Massey, artist, sculptor, and children's book author, and Bernie Massey, director of the Center for

American Studies and Culture. The project entailed replacing the deteriorating eighteen-year-old painted polyvinyl-coated sound-insulating blankets (PVC) that covered the exterior of the oil derrick with new PVC sound-insulation blankets painted by over three thousand hospitalized children. The derrick has two layers of blankets, but the project only affected the outer layer because of their poor condition. Painted blankets on each of the four sides represent one of the four seasons. A floral motif was conceived because flowers give life, beautify, and symbolize hope. The artwork transformed the tower into an artistic monument.

With the exception of installation, all work was done off-site. Project coordinators delivered materials to hospitals and cancer camps throughout the state and the children worked with professional artists to paint the blankets with the aid of stencils. Any child who wished to participate was included. Special paintbrushes were made for children missing limbs and the effort was called, "inspirational" by most participants.

The panels were installed with the use of cranes and there were changes in elevations to the derrick structure. The tower, taller than the Statue of Liberty, has three times the painting area of the Sistine Chapel ceiling and necessitated the efforts of over forty thousand volunteers.

It is not unusual for oil facilities to go unnoticed or to be disguised from public view. Most citizens would be shocked by the volume of oil production daily in the Los Angeles Basin, unaware until necessity or publicity demands. The BreitBurn Energy facility at Pico Boulevard and Doheny Drive is contained within the walls of what appears to be an office building or school. Many residents in the area would never imagine its true nature. The Beverly Center shopping mall on San Vicente and La Cienega Boulevard between Beverly and Third Street sits next to a full-scale working oil derrick and rig in plain view. It is located on the San Vicente side and covered only by a half-wall, yet the majority would drive by and never notice its presence. On Wilshire Boulevard stand the La Brea Tar Pits as a testament to the existence of oil since prehistoric times. Oil puddles up from the pits, providing a popular tourist destination for visitors throughout the world. If the public is oblivious to oil derricks in their midst, it may be because they are simply too busy to notice.

Once Erin Brockovich's allegations became public, attention was focused on a facility that had previously operated in relative anonymity. Despite the highly visible nature of the derrick, it commanded little notice from either residents or students and had become as comfortable as an old hutch taking up space in Grandma's dining room. Notwithstanding occasional complaints about noxious smells on the field, the derrick existed in a haze of obscurity.

Sudden fame brought new concerns. In the space of only a few months the large flowered tower became the high-profile target of everyone's fear and loathing. Within a few weeks Venoco Inc. was cited for illegally venting gas and in April noticed for a faulty amine unit that initiated a shutdown. The timing could not have been worse. These incidents heightened fear within a community already terrified Brockovich's claims might be true.

Throughout the duration of the lawsuit, despite constant questions about why no testing had been done, the answer remained the same: We didn't know it was dangerous. We thought the authorities were overseeing the site. There were agencies that were supposed to be watching and we assumed . . . Was this the party line or actually the sum total of the city's past environmental attitude? Could it simply have been a desire to allay any crisis of conscience for those who had enabled the well's existence for so long? Or had the city actually done was what necessary through the years to address occasional complaints and issues as they arose?

In an effort to discern the truth, I spoke with three educators familiar with the early history of the issues. According to them, throughout the 1970s and '80s the schools were faced with occasional oil situations they placated and addressed quickly and quietly. Staff attempting to deal individually with those few early problems perceived the school administrators as eager to control both the information and solutions.

Smells from the oil well were widely regarded with dismay and many community members admitted they voiced concerns throughout the years. When teachers placed calls to the oil company, they were directed to address their questions and concerns to the school administration. Coach Susan Stevens spoke candidly about the concerns she and other high-level physical education staff experienced through the years. "We did not have a hotline to call concerning the noxious odors on the field. If we needed to let someone know that the odor was strong, we called our principal's office and they contacted the company. None of us recalls these incidents happening too many times and I do not think they kept a list of any of those calls."

Stevens could not personally recall anyone becoming sick as a result of those odors. "I do not know of anyone getting ill. It did not happen enough [to be memorable], but we might have. We did not allow the students to run if there was too strong a smell on a particular day."

Aside from the illnesses attributed to the campus, Stevens spoke philosophically about the dangers of Los Angeles air, saying, "As far as what contributes most to the acceptance of bad air quality, I just think that living in Los Angeles one has to accept the air quality or move. We were more concerned about the smog levels back in the '70s than anything else."

She admits she cannot imagine doing anything differently. "As I said, even being told about the oil well, I still would have taught at the high school. The gals I talked to and I all remember that the oil well was very close to the school. We all remember how the balls went over the fence and the man who was in the oil well area would throw the balls not covered with too much oil back over to us." In the early years Coach Stevens recalls having to contend with several such "inconveniences" caused by the well. She also remembers an open pit on the soccer field filled with sludge that became a magnet for balls on a daily basis.

The well was moved and reconfigured in the mid- to late 1970s to allow for more drilling. "Where the well was located is now part of the upper field, which is used all of the time. The [physical education] department was probably not involved in the decision to move it and the one lady who might know is not doing well health-wise, so would not be able to help on this."

How does Coach Stevens feel now about the well's placement so near a school? "I would say that the oil well ought not to be there. That would be in a perfect world. The air quality is better now than in the '70s, but of course is not what we might like it to be.

"As far as the number of teachers getting sick—within the physical education department—lots of people taught with us throughout the years. When I started in 1971 there were eighteen teachers in our department. There were a few who did get cancer. I do not know if it had anything to do with teaching physical education. There is a study being done on teachers and health conducted by people at USC. It is called the California Teachers Study and they did find that there were higher incidences of certain cancers in all teachers and less of other types of cancers in teachers than the population at large. The study is ongoing." Coach Stevens explained the testing was not specific to the Beverly Hills well site and she knew of no excess cancer studies concerning teachers in the district.

Responding to the issue of noxious odors, Venoco vice president Mike Edwards explained the cause. "The gas company adds the odorant (typically a 'mercaptan,' or methylmercaptan) at the transfer point (inside our wall) so the natural gas will have a distinct odor." Edwards said that would help identify any leaks or problems.

In addition to the localized smells and goo on Beverly Hills' playground, the entire Southern California area was under a constant barrage of particulates and poisons that brought citizens to their feet and running indoors to escape. Air quality during the 1970s existed at such dangerous levels, smog alerts were a regular event and it was not uncommon to see masks covering the mouths of people as they went about their daily routines. When residents responded to Erin Brockovich's claims, many willingly admitted air problems were widespread throughout the Los Angeles area and not a localized issue.

One fact is certain about Beverly Hills High School: it was and still is dedicated to sports. Principal Ben Bushman was devoted to athletics and the field played a significant part in the daily activities at the high school. In a recent conversation with Bushman, he reiterated his belief that the city and schools had acted responsibly in all matters concerning the wells: "When we received a complaint we always followed up." Bushman said they never saw any problems they were unable to address or fix. He believed there was a desire by the oil company to be cooperative and responsive whenever notified.

.

Bushman said despite occasional concerns from parents or teachers, he dealt with any issues in a timely manner.

Margaret Leeds was department chairperson and an assistant principal who served at BHHS from 1960 to 1995. According to Leeds, a chain of command was set up to deal with the oil wells in the 1970s. "The administration told us if there were a problem with the well not to call the company directly but to report it to the principal." Leeds said the district wanted to deal with the issue because there were twenty or thirty people teaching or coaching in the field area and directing concerns through the principal would expedite the process.

She also vividly remembers an open pit filled with sludge that was a problem for archery classes and volleyballs. "I don't know what emitted from it, but when the field was reconfigured it was put underground." Leeds recalled what she calls "functioning at a different level in those days." Pipes, sludge, and open, messy pits were accepted as part of the work process and she, as well as most others, trusted it was safe. "When there are more cancers, and these things are on your mind you become more aware of the environment, what is on your skin and body, and you become more concerned, and then aggressively deal with it. At that time it was just an inconvenience and one thing we dealt with." Eventually Leeds said the open pit behind the bleachers on the north end of the archery field was moved, and all the oil wells were relocated to the end of the field to allow the women more asphalt area.

Leeds admits they didn't question higher-ups in those days and environmental concerns were discussed less. "We had a department chair, Barbara Wilson, who wanted everything to be perfect with the administration. She was on top of everything, even small things like when a P.E. teacher wanted to go the office, we had to change clothes first. It was a different era in terms of measuring the girls' skirts from hem to ground. We didn't question authority and we were expected not to rock the boat, but I kept asking questions until I got answers."

She continues, "I remember seeing the steam from Sempra [Energy's power plant] and it was noisy at times. They explained this was caused when they backwashed the filters when they were bad. We keep learning more so we can make it better for the next generation. The better way to do that is through collaboration, not litigation."

Not everyone felt the way Leeds did. The lawyers continued to enlist plaintiffs and each time Erin spoke about an abundance of cancers my phone rang with questions from parents about the well safety. Should they pull their children out of school, was the air toxic, could their kids have already been harmed? Did I know anything new that could help them decide what they should do? Most were in panic mode; all were eager to receive factual information.

Although my only response could be to wait for the test results and let the science provide answers, I personally experienced decidedly mixed reactions. I felt anger yet was still uncertain at whom it should be directed. Were the anxiety and fear in these parents and children the result of environmental outlaws, Erin's attempt to exploit the Beverly Hills name, or the city and school board's failure to protect the community? I wasn't even close to answering these questions, nor was anyone else at that point.

City and school officials were also angry, but to their credit they strengthened their resolve and moved forward to test and to reassure the community they were doing everything possible to uncover the truth.

The apparent wrinkles in the fabric of Beverly Hills' peace of mind were highlighted by a vast number of unanswered questions the new citations inspired. The amine unit incident shone a spotlight on the community's inability to comprehend the scientific complexities at the high-school campus and raised new fears about potential dangers to students' health. As with most of the city at that time, I did not know that an amine unit is a device used to remove carbon dioxide and help clean natural gas prior to delivering it to the gas company. Following a source and amine unit inspection of the facility by the Air Quality Management District, elevated benzene levels were discovered. It was decided the existing unit would not comply with the rules on a consistent basis and Sam Atwood of the AQMD recommended upgrading the equipment to minimize the pollution risk.

Atwood informed me that Venoco had received two tickets since the amine unit was closed off, which totaled three that year. The first was in February for improper venting. While those tickets were under review at the AQMD legal department, AQMD denied Venoco's application for an amine unit permit and halted operations. Atwood explained the decision, saying, "We shut them down and they had to reapply for a new permit with a considerably enhanced pollution control and monitoring system that would ensure their benzene emissions in the future would be so low the resulting risk would not be significant."

Venoco was ordered to provide a health risk assessment of the site, but company vice president Edwards claimed no analysis could be done until the wells once again became operational. Atwood said a health risk assessment would be a valuable, scientific tool to accompany extensive air testing by the AQMD and by the city's consultants. He said no assessment had been done previously because past reports gave no indication to suspect they were exceeding limits. Now, however, based on current figures gathered around the southern part of the state, they wanted to ensure Venoco was not exceeding the limits for benzene emissions.

Parents like Jody Kleinman questioned the production and gas levels at the wells, worrying that there could be illegal venting again. "I want to know what happens to the gas after Venoco meets its quota. What do they do with the excess?"

Edwards explained the process by which Venoco gauges its gas production. "The amount of oil produced is related to the amount of gas the gas company will buy," Edwards said. "Natural gas is a byproduct of the oil production. We have to make sure our oil production is limited so that we don't produce more natural gas than our daily sales volume will allow." Edwards said computers calculate the rate, which is consistent for production to remain at a certain level. "We have a daily limit. We will produce at a certain rate that is within sales limitations. Our sales contract specifies the amount the gas company will buy and we want to keep the production going, not start and stop the pumps. All the wells flow into one area to calculate the total volume. Then they flow into a separator to separate the gas from the liquid. Liquids are separated into water and oil, with the water going into a reinjection well and the oil into a pipeline that flows to a Long Beach refinery. The gas goes into the gas company's gas distribution line off of Olympic Boulevard."

Although the AQMD completed their review of the permit for Venoco's amine unit and ultimately decided it met all their rules and standards, they opted not to request an environmental study. Due to the proximity of the equipment to the high school, it was, however, subject to rule 212 which required a thirty-day public notice period prior to the final issuance of the permit. Venoco was ordered to prepare a health risk assessment under regulation 1402 of the South Coast Air Quality Management District. The public notice had to be distributed by Venoco to each parent or legal guardian of children in any school within a quarter mile of the facility and to each address within a one-thousand-foot radius of the outer property line of the facility. The company was required to provide proof of notifications and method to the AQMD. The AQMD denied Venoco a permit to reopen until the thirty-day comment period ended and a health risk assessment of the site was performed.

Hundreds of residents responded to the outreach, voicing concerns and opinions about well safety issues. When asked how the public comments would affect the process, AQMD executive Barry Wallerstein was forthcoming: "It's not whether or not the public wants the well, but comments providing any additional information pertaining to the approval of the amine unit approval specifically."

Atwood admitted that although many of the comments from parents urged closure of Venoco operations, no significant legal grounds existed to prevent the company from resuming production once the amine unit was replaced and complied with AQMD standards. It became quickly apparent to anyone paying attention that closing down an existing oil well was indeed a formidable task unless evidence could be found to prove a serious health threat. It also fueled fears Brockovich's claims may be founded in truth and gave her more ammunition in the public relations war.

Testing of the site with the faulty amine unit had sounded a call for alarm from parents who believed the allegations. It also raised some suspicion in those who hadn't thus far bought into Masry's claims. The risk numbers were high, 81.7 parts per million on two days in April 2003, for example, when the carbon filter in the amine unit was not functioning properly.

Atwood addressed these high numbers in terms of cancer risk. "This carbon filter is like the one in your home or your car. When it gets filled after collecting the gunk, it no longer functions properly. Then it must be changed out and replaced. We believe when the amine unit was placed in operation the carbon unit was functioning properly and filtering out benzene, but that over time, the carbon unit became saturated and needed to be changed." Atwood said he believed the unit had been operating ineffectively over a short period of time, maybe weeks or months at most.

This attempt to pacify parents did not allay the fears of a community frightened and angry and now in possession of tangible proof a problem actually existed. Former BHHS student Ari Bussel challenged Atwood's belief, voicing the opinion of many other alumni at that point in time: "He believes there was a problem, but why was it not checked on a regular basis? How can one trust his 'belief,' which conveniently serves him when a problem surfaces?"

The AQMD visited the site during this period to do several ambient air tests and on April 30, when the new carbon filter was connected, the benzene levels dropped to less than .1 parts per million. "We have constructed the amine unit so as to virtually eliminate actual emissions," Edwards said. "The calculated level of emissions in the AQMD notice is based on a gas rate that is three times our actual production. Our staff estimated the worst case potential cancer risk over a 70-year lifetime, 24 hours a day, 365 days per year at 0.03 in one million, which is well below any agency threshold."

Wallerstein echoed Edwards: "Venoco was well below any

agency's threshold of significant risk for toxic air emissions for the amine unit." Atwood added, "One other thing to note is that gas is vented from a very tall stack [165 feet high] and we don't believe there is a danger when released from that height."

Follow-up ambient air testing in April showed levels of benzene at the site testing lower than levels across the state. However, the good news did little to appease Jody Kleinman, who had been made livid by the violations. "They can claim it was only malfunctioning for a short period, but since they never tested, how would they possibly know or determine the time span of the higher emission levels? What possible excuse could justify any higher readings at any time on our campus? This just validates the fact no industrial site is appropriate at a school and only enhances the risk of exposure to harmful chemicals. Any extra toxins for any length of time are unacceptable when it comes to our children."

New fear arose with regard to well safety after an AQMD memo surfaced in 2004. In a note written on February 12, 2003, by AQMD employee Katsumi Keeler to coworker Ben Shaw, Keeler wrote, "Although the unit operator cinched down on the hatches, I can't stress enough that this is becoming an immediate health and safety issue, not because of chronic effects, but due to the possibility of explosion. Honestly, I may be overstating the hazards here—after all, the Gas Company has blocked off on them in the past. However, on previous occasions, the off-gasses [the evaporation of chemicals or VOCs released into the air] were stacked. Therefore, I think we have to act with an abundance of caution here."

Keeler added his opinion that the Beverly Hills Fire Department should be notified. In a memo from Inspector Pang Mueller on Wednesday, February 12, 2003, to Dr. Wallerstein and Mohzen Nazerri, AQMD engineer, Keeler wrote, "Please note that District

Prosecutor Peter Mieras called the Beverly Hills Fire Department this morning to report our inspection results and asked them to take appropriate actions to protect public safety."

The Beverly Hills Fire Department has two sources of response. One is through dispatch, the other through the fire marshal, who annually checks the site. According to the fire marshal, no call was made by the AQMD to him personally and dispatch could not check the records. Although a request was made shortly after the report surfaced, it could never be discovered if the memo had any true validity. Whether a call came in was only known by the fire department and the records, to this day have been unavailable.

Bussel responded to the memo, asking, "If a responsible inspector calls the attention to a possible hazard, why was it not followed up? Why is there no procedure requiring someone to follow up and put a checkmark, noting who was notified, when, and what action was taken?"

Atwood commented following the incident that it was important to bear in mind the report addressed the opinion of one inspector and there were other things to consider as well. "Venoco itself has two alarms if the gas reaches an explosive limit in close proximity to the amine unit. Neither was activated that night, although the inspector, for whatever reasons, believed there was an explosive hazard. We notified the fire department about the findings."

Edwards verified they were moving forward with safety precautions at the site. "In accordance with the agreement with the SCAQMD [South Coast Air Quality Management District] last October, rupture disks and sensors were installed on the piping leading to the vent stack to alert operators if gas is vented. Venoco is required to notify the SCAQMD as soon as possible (within one hour) if the disk ruptures.

"In the absence of actual test data, the SCAQMD properly erred on the side of caution, but actual air quality testing by the SCAQMD on our site (in close proximity to oil/ water separation area) on six different occasions, as well as independent air quality testing conducted by a consultant to the City of Beverly Hills, shows air quality was normal."

Edwards said Venoco would continue to comply and provide factual information on the quality of the air on and around the site. "We will also cooperate in other scientific investigations to assist everyone concerned in determining what is and what is not a health concern. To that end, a health risk assessment is being prepared and will be submitted to the SCAQMD by the end of March.

"Additionally, a fence line monitor will be installed by mid-April to measure any produced gas that is emitted from our facility. A wind monitor will be installed to correlate data from the fence line monitor."

Atwood of the AQMD assured the city that the well's east and north fence lines would measure hydrocarbons, including methane, and that the continuous measuring at the two locations on the site were a condition for resuming oil production. A separate monitor attached to the amine unit itself would measure benzene levels and a meteorological monitor would be located elsewhere on the field.

Skeptical parents remained unsatisfied with these changes and Jody Kleinman reiterated her responsibility to protect her child. The violations by Venoco had sown seeds of distrust and harvested fear among many. Kleinman stated, "All the issues being raised now only leave me more concerned about the scientific truths and the ability of the regulatory agencies to properly monitor and analyze the data so crucial to our children's safety."

Venoco was once again up and running, but so were concerned parents. The negative information combined with new revelations relating to Venoco forced the school district to pursue more aggressive methods to allay the community's fears. It seemed the meetings about the site became nonstop both publicly and privately whenever a potential problem arose.

Despite the mixed response from the public, Edwards was confident the new measures sufficiently addressed monitoring issues and should suffice to put parents' minds at ease over safety. "The data will be captured and recorded instantaneously on a computerized system. In talking with BHHS parent Jody Kleinman about the new continuous air monitoring system, I emphasized it is in our best interest to have scientifically valid data. We will work with the AQMD to ensure that it is accurately collected and accurately reported. Additionally, the AQMD can inspect the equipment or audit the data at any time." Venoco was also formulating a plan to be submitted to the AQMD addressing concerns about site data accumulation.

Edwards added that safety systems were already in place, including fire detectors, a suppression system, and lower explosive limit monitors that monitored gas accumulations. Additionally, new methods of monitoring would identify low hydrocarbon concentrations and employing technologies both currently in use and planned for the Alaskan oil fields, these safeguards ensured detection before gas could reach dangerous levels. One such new method passed a beam of infrared light along the fenced perimeter and the refraction from the light beam detected hydrocarbon emissions. Edwards assured parents that although it had not yet been instituted in Alaska, it had already been proven effective.

If hydrocarbon emissions exceeded acceptable AQMD levels, Venoco would be required to notify the agency within one hour's time of release of unpermitted oil field gas from the facility. Venoco was also required to maintain monitoring records for five years and make them available to the AQMD. In addition to the $60,000 monitoring cost, the company was ordered to pay a $10,000 fine.

Atwood required Venoco to begin testing immediately to determine the ratio of benzene to other volatile organic compounds (VOCs) to establish the benzene concentration. There is a threshold limit of four parts per million and that level is equivalent to one in one millionth cancer risk. "Our regulatory limit is twenty-five in one million, so if their health risk assessment shows greater than twenty-five to one million risk they will have to reduce that risk, depending on the risk location," Atwood added.

"This permit lays out some very stringent conditions for operation of the well facility and we are watching closely to make sure they abide by the conditions," Atwood said. "If they don't, we are issuing multiple notices and we have the capability of going to the AQMD Hearing Board and seeking an order which would compel the facility to abide by all regulations by deadlines. If all other measures fail, they have the authority to shut down the operation." Atwood warned there would be no "wiggle room" in the agreement and Venoco would have six months to submit a monitoring plan to the AQMD for data collection.

Edwards stated his belief that the monitoring would prove beneficial to all concerned. "In community meetings and subsequent discussions with local residents, we have repeatedly heard that continuous air monitoring at our site is a very important issue. We are pleased that most of the financial settlement goes directly to installing this equipment."

Amid the storm of controversy surrounding the site, students were experiencing their own deep frustration over their fate. New awareness of issues concerning illegal venting and amine units, combined with VOC levels, was unsettling and highly confusing to residents. Cancer risks and parts per million fell short of the words residents longed to hear: the wells are completely safe. Although parents expressed the most concerns, the student body opened another front in the battle for more information. The student newspaper, *The Norman News,* published articles and the high-school underground newspaper, *The Beverly Underground,* was vocal in its opposition and investigation of the site. It produced numerous articles and did some quite admirable investigative reporting on the issue.

Although nothing was ever sufficiently proven to validate the claims that past errors had been the cause of the health issues, some students and parents opted to leave Beverly for other schools. I interviewed five BHHS students who declined use of their names but spoke candidly about their fears. The level of frustration was even more apparent by the lack of concrete information and the ongoing battle of words between the lawyers and the city.

Student A had already registered for the GED (General Equivalency Degree) and would be attending Santa Monica College (SMC) in lieu of graduating from Beverly Hills High. "I am an honors student in AP [advanced placement] classes and I don't want to leave high school; this is my senior year. But I am afraid of staying and getting cancer.

"I signed up for the GED test for November and seven or eight of my friends are taking it also. I know about twenty in all who are leaving. I will transfer to SMC and graduate from there, then go on to UCLA or whatever."

Asked about the field, she said she was on the cross-country team in ninth grade. "I didn't even know about the oil well then or what it was, but I could smell it—like something was burning or like gas."

Student B explained her family was still debating whether or not to stay and had not reached a decision. "You just don't feel safe or secure there. The majority of the school doesn't feel safe. At first it seemed like a movie: not true or a dream. When you think about going to Beverly Hills schools and what it's like to live here and its reputation. I spent so many years on the track, doing sports and fulfilling my requirements, plus my extracurricular activities. To think I could get a disease for that, it's outrageous."

Student B noted they had attended Erin Brockovich's initial meeting and listened carefully to all the information. "She [Erin] told us all these alarming facts and the other side says it's safe and I say fine, you can't look into things so much. Is this desk totally clean? Nothing is perfect. I don't know what to believe; I'm caught in the middle between two sides."

She was frustrated and added that she did not feel comfortable with an oil field beneath her and her fellow students. "This doesn't seem right, to have the field here under the school. My parents and I and my friends, we talk about whether it's worth it to leave or stay and see what happens. It's such a predicament. Should I leave or take a chance and stay, and what if it turns out to be bad?"

As of that time, student B had not signed up for the GED. "I feel that I have never sloughed off in high school and I want to see what colleges I can get into. During the summer we were having an ongoing argument. I wanted to stay, but my parents are afraid for me and they want me to apply to private schools."

Student C also agonized over her decision to stay and finish senior year. "It's my senior year and I feel like I should finish here, but truthfully I am very uncomfortable and every day I am here and I run on the track, it worries me. If I were younger I would leave, but at this point it would be detrimental to my education.

"I have been applying to schools and I have good grades. Overall, my years at Beverly have been good, but this has tainted my high-school experience. Every time and every day I am running on the track, I think about this. I run by the oil well and I am reminded. And there is nothing I can do, so it frustrates me. My parents are worried, just like I am, but it's obviously too late now to leave. If I was younger, I'd go, but no one really knows now, do they?"

Student D had already transferred out of Beverly and noted she was deeply depressed. "I have a great love for Beverly High and I have been going through so many emotional phases since this started. Every day when I have to go to my new school and try to adjust to the new surroundings, I feel sad. When I see my friends and am reminded of what I left behind, I am depressed for days and I sob at night.

"My parents told me I could come back to Beverly if I was so unhappy, but I don't know if it's safe. I just don't feel comfortable. I want to come back desperately, but then I remember last year, when I had to hold my breath when I ran around the track and how I pleaded with the teacher not to make me run on the field. I would hold my breath, but you can't do that for long, so I would hold my nose and try not to breathe.

"The oil problem at the high school has ruined my life and scratched my soul deeply. I'm scared of becoming a cancer victim even though I want to go back to Beverly desperately."

Student D's parents said they felt bad for their child, but with all the multiple problems at the school—aside from Venoco, they feared Sempra—they just did not feel comfortable. They said their child could come back, but the torment of not knowing what to do depressed them further. "I can't explain what an impact it's had on my child," Student

D's mother said. "She loved this school and it was one of the best schools to attend you could ever ask for."

All four students agreed that the only way they would ever feel safe again was with the closure of the well. After these and other conversations with students, I was acutely aware of how the allegations were impacting the lives of young people who should be enjoying their high-school years free from worries about VOCs, diseases, and oil regulations. Clearly the allegations had caused great disruption to people's lives and well-being. Too many said the incident would alter the memories of their years at Beverly forever.

However, a fifth student expressed an opposite response to the issue. Student E explained, "I never worried about the wells. I thought it was silly because there are so many different oil wells all over the area and I never heard of anything causing a problem. I never gave it a second thought and I am an athlete and run the field. My close friends are not concerned either, but I know there are some who are. A kid I know quit the team because of the wells. This hasn't impacted on my experience at Beverly and I am not worried about the wells or any health risk."

Throughout the ongoing debates over well safety, the school board and the city continually maintained their confidence in the findings, but disgruntled parents addressed the city council to voice concern over the Venoco-AQMD settlement. "What good is this if we find out there were problems after the fact and our kids have already been exposed?" Mahshid Soleimani asked. "Every step of the way is better than nothing, but it doesn't give me increased confidence that our children and teachers are safe." Nooshin Meshkaty added her concerns, stating, "Some of you are attorneys. . . . If these children were your clients, you would find a way to get the wells shut down."

Minor problems continued to focus attention on the site. In 2005 the fence line monitors erupted after an oil spill raised emissions levels during a routine maintenance operation. Edwards said the AQMD had been notified and inspected the problem, but no violation or fines were issued.

According to Mohsen Nazimi, deputy executive officer of Engineering and Compliance for the AQMD, the Venoco site has additional safety obligations. "Because of the sensitivity of this site and concerns expressed by the parents, we have imposed a number of extra requirements on Venoco and as a result, we have additional bells and whistles like the fence line monitor. However, the level of notification we elected for the fence line monitor was set for a level we felt was health protective with the intent they notify us when they are doing something that would cause an excess."

When the spill occurred Venoco was undergoing maintenance at 8:18 A.M. and the pressure of the wells built up, causing a little less than a barrel (42 gallons) of oil to squirt out of the well. The majority of the 42 gallons of oil landed on the ground inside the pitching cage on the high-school field, directly adjacent to the block wall separating the properties. There was also some oil on the metal bars that constitute the cage roof. Absorbent pads were used to soak up the oil then the top layer of dirt in the area was scraped. BHHS principal Dan Stepenosky told the AQMD he received no complaints from students or teachers about the incident.

Nazimi said the problem was brought under control within 20 minutes, but Venoco was required to take certain preventative measures, such as immediate air sampling with a Summa canister that was sent to the lab for analysis. "We received no complaints about odors at the site or any other nuisance problem," Nazimi continued. "The important thing was that Venoco notify us within the hour time frame and they did so."

He didn't believe there was any significant air quality impact or immediate health issues caused by the spill. "There was no reason to pull kids off the playground because we had no complaints about odors. We don't have any requirement that Venoco notify the schools or city; it's for them to arrange between themselves."

Edwards said the fence line monitors' infrared system detects hydrocarbons as they pass through and the warning system is then set off and sends an alert. Venoco claims detection levels are set at extremely low emissions, so there is no danger if the monitor is activated. "The monitor had discontinued activation by the time the AQMD inspector arrived," Edwards said.

At one time these incidents would have passed unnoticed. Now Kleinman and others viewed the situation differently. "I want all parents and community members to be told what really happened while our children were at school last Thursday. Venoco oil production facilities on our school campus failed once again to operate properly. The fence line monitor only alerted officials *after* unsafe gases and toxic chemicals had been released. What do I say to my child? How do I explain that I was not informed? Do I answer by telling her that our city's municipal code [Section 10-5.306C] specifically states that in consideration of the health and welfare of the citizens, a production facility of this type may operate nowhere else in Beverly Hills, with the exception of her high-school campus? Shame on all of us for that answer."

Kleinman believed the spill once again validated her claim that the Venoco operation was a risky and completely unacceptable use of school grounds. "An oil production facility simply should not be allowed to operate in close proximity to our children. All necessary steps to permanently close Venoco down should be taken."

Despite the spillage, with the exception of Kleinman most parents were silent and expressed no concern, at least to me. At a certain point the entire dynamic seemed to shift, and an attitude of lethargy and acceptance overtook the community. I am not certain there was one incident that convinced residents that concern over the wells was unnecessary, but I began to notice a dramatic change in the community's attention level. The first evidence of indifference followed the first of what would be a series of articles noting the presence of the commonly used chemical hexavalent chromium, or chromium six, at the site. Sempra and others had been using the chemical until its use was outlawed the late 1980s and early 1990s.

Chromium six is a dangerous toxin. It is used in industry for the production of stainless steel, textile dyes, paints, and plastics, as well as wood preservation and leather tanning. Inhaled hexavalent chromium is recognized by the CDC and the EPA as a human carcinogen, but it has other acute and chronic health affects, targeting mostly the respiratory tract. Its use as a rust inhibitor in industrial facilities made it prevalent and widespread in schools and office buildings. New studies are uncovering its dangers when ingested as well, yet it is still found in drinking water.

The toxin achieved fame on the national scene when it appeared in Erin Brockovich's movie about Hinkley, California's water supply. Erin alleged the chemical was the cause of cancer and tumors in the residents and filed suit against Pacific Gas & Electric for leeching it into the water. The allegations in that case became legendary and still serve to foster Brockovich's reputation and authenticity despite her repeated failures to repeat her success in other locations.

I was certain my headline declaring that it had been part of the Beverly Hills airscape at Sempra would elicit a deluge of calls, but I heard from no one. That was when I suspected the City of Beverly Hills was officially "over" Erin Brockovich.

4

The Scent on Rodeo Drive

The general who wins the battle makes many calculations in his temple before the battle is fought. The general who loses makes but few calculations beforehand.

—Sun Tzu

After Brockovich's test results came to light, the city moved forward with a dual purpose: to appease concerned parents by hiring an independent testing firm and to circle the wagons and do battle against the onslaught of trial lawyers focused on Beverly Hills' deep pockets. To keep their word to the residents, the city council retained the services of Camp, Dresser, and McKee (CDM), who would test air and soil gases. Simultaneously, school board president Barry Brucker announced that the school board and city council had signed a joint defense agreement against the anticipated Masry & Vititoe litigation. According to City Attorney Larry Wiener, the agreement allowed shared confidentiality. This arrangement permitted both sets of attorneys to communicate and maintain attorney-client privilege since both expected to be named in lawsuits.

Councilmembers assured the community that CDM was

a worldwide concern specializing in geological investigations and testing. The company is comprised of teams of award-winning scientists in their respective fields and attorney Larry Wiener was assigned as a go-between. Among those recruited within CDM were the vice president and senior hydrogeologist Steven L. Brewer, senior air quality engineer John R. Person, senior hydrogeologist Thomas D. Blackman, senior project manager Ravi Subramanian, and environmental scientist Angela K. Patterson. They would lead and initiate investigation of everything pertaining to the oil fields at the high school and examine all aspects for problems regarding soil, water, or air quality. When the hire was announced, City Manager Mark Scott promised, "The results of the tests will be shared with the entire community."

This goal of transparency would not prove as reassuring to all parents as the city had hoped, and testing progressed with a certain degree of controversy. Erin and her team remained adamant her original results were the accurate assessment of the air quality and cause of the health issues. The city's experts, CDM and the AQMD, returned normal levels with each new study. Occasionally, a certain chemical would show an elevated reading but could not be duplicated with further tests, nor could their presence be explained. Acetone and toluene seemed most often problematic, but no direct cause or explanation was ever offered for the spike.

To many community members the situation extended beyond hiring testing companies and checking air quality. They were insisting on action and time after time at council meetings a dedicated group of parents articulated their fears. Some urged the school to immediately shut down the oil wells at the BHHS site. Others advocated buying out Venoco.

One parent and former student suffering from non-Hodgkin's

lymphoma voiced concern the school board and city would suffer financial repercussions if the wells remained operational. "Until the closed ranks open up and [we] find out what's in the air and in the soil, our economy will take a nose dive," she said. "When I think how much good could be done by closing down that 'darn cute little oil well with the flowers'! We're all concerned parents and we care about school safety. Our job and mandate is to secure the safety and well-being of all our kids. What I'm hearing tonight is a need for more work on our communication skills."

Two parents that evening stepped forward and announced they had pulled their son from baseball because they were distrustful of air safety on the field. However, not all parents agreed there was an imminent danger. Elizabeth Chait, parent and former student, voiced her confidence the field was safe. "I attended the high school and was on the track all the time. I am fine and I am sure it is safe for my children to be there."

At one meeting, Michael Karlin stepped up to applaud the school board's efforts in a difficult situation, quoting Mark Twain: "Common sense ain't so common." Praising the board for being the voice of the people, Karlin said, "They are not getting paid here. They are also parents and I am absolutely persuaded that all of them have concerns and we have to give them the trust and respect they deserve for doing a good job. They are us."

The meetings were always split with each side certain its opinion was the correct one. The fact that so many alumni still reside in the city and are raising their children in Beverly Hills created an odd paradox. Scores of residents believed the well was safe and they had not suffered any ill effects from attending the school. Others were adamant there was a danger and the well should be removed. Everyone was on one side or the other but no one was neutral on the subject.

As time passed and more testing returned safe levels, the number of parents at council and school board meetings diminished. Soon it was only a handful who even took the time to show up and focus a spotlight on the issue.

Superintendent Dr. Gwen Gross would issue a statement at the beginning of most school board meetings in an attempt to allay parental concern. It was also hoped it would ward off any arguments from disgruntled parents. One typical statement read:

> As you know, when the potential for risk was first alleged, we immediately began working with the Air Quality Management District (AQMD), who is charged with monitoring oil well emissions and who conducted a series of tests.
>
> So far, the data collected by the South Coast Air Quality Management District tells a different story from what has been presented by the attorneys, who are soliciting clients in the community.
>
> The South Coast Air Quality Management District conducted a series of tests on three separate occasions in February to determine the level of various air pollutants at the high school and adjacent sites.
>
> On February 6th, the AQMD took a series of air samples to determine the level of several air pollutants.
>
> On February 15th, the AQMD took additional outdoor air samples at three locations: Beverly Hills High, on the property of Venoco and at Roxbury Park.
>
> On February 28th, the AQMD took additional air samples at two locations within the high school, the property of Venoco and Roxbury Park.
>
> To quote directly from the memo of AQMD Executive Officer Dr. Barry Wallerstein, "To date, monitoring at the high school area has not shown readings of benzene, hexane

and other air toxic levels that are considered abnormal." In fact, according to the District's consultant, the levels are "well below" what the California Environmental Protection Agency Office of Environmental Health Hazard Assessment deems to be the minimum exposure levels for public safety. The AQMD conducted more comprehensive tests this month, and we expect those results in coming weeks. The District is aware of several parents' interest in hiring their own environmental consultants. Related to that, we think it is critically important to coordinate efforts with parents. We are all after the same information. What we think would be constructive is for the parents to meet with the City and the District to discuss these issues, and we are prepared to set up that meeting immediately.

Our overriding concern is the health and safety of Beverly Hills High School students, teachers, staff, administrators and local residents. That has guided our efforts thus far, and it will continue to guide our efforts from this point forward.

Venoco vice president Mike Edwards confirmed the company was still relying on the AQMD results at the site. Edwards also pointed out that Venoco has never been in control of or owned the abandoned underground oil wells—remnants of a previous oil company lease—located on another part of the field. "We understand that parents are looking for answers and we can appreciate the concern they have for their children's health. Venoco will continue to cooperate with the AQMD on any additional air quality testing and is open to cooperating with the air quality testing that includes interested parties and that follows strict, scientific testing procedures."

When Dr. Wallerstein of the AQMD wasn't able to complete final testing on the wells because they were not fully operational, having been shut off by Venoco that spring to fix the amine unit, he released a statement to the residents. "I was invited by

the Beverly Hills Board of Education President Barry Brucker
to come and speak before the Board and as soon as the wells
are fully operational and the final testing is done, I will come
and disclose all of our findings to the board."

Even with the continued efforts to answer questions and
reduce the disruptions the wells posed, Dr. Gross believed the
issue was creating a heavy weight for the district to bear. No
one could argue that confusion reigned regarding whether or
not Brockovich's alleged tests had actually picked up readings
others were missing. Were the state agencies testing in the
right places and could they be trusted? Skeptics remained
difficult to persuade.

Despite the district's constant attempts to calm fears, a
parent-driven petition to close the wells garnered more than
two thousand names. Circulated by BHHS parent Mahshid
Soleimani, it urged the city to turn off the pumps for good
and alleged that the reports of the city's environmental
consultants, CDM, showed oil and gas production did impact
air quality at the school. Soleimani was extremely passionate
in her concerns. She was particularly upset over the higher
levels of toluene and acetone at the sight and believed the city
was hiding information. The bulk of the Iranian American
community, a large group within Beverly Hills, seemed to
agree with her assessment of the situation.

Frustration over the lack of answers she sought was obvious,
and I am not certain her fears have ever been allayed. Her
history seemed to factor into her government mistrust. I did
note on many occasions a difference in philosophy toward
government by Mahshid Soleimani and other Beverly Hills
parents of Persian origin. The Persian community appeared
far less willing to believe the council and city officials or
take them at their word than did their non-Middle Eastern

counterparts. I noted a mistrust of the system and it was interesting how many more native-born Americans at that time readily accepted official explanations than those who had lived under less open and democratic regimes.

Beverly Hills mayor Jimmy Delshad, himself of Persian descent, explained such attitudes: "They do not trust government statements because of two cultural reasons. One is not being very active in city government and two, not trusting any government. For example, witness what is going on now in Iran; multiply this mistrust by a factor of ten when it could affect the well-being of their children."

The Persian community was not alone in its misgivings regarding the local government's response, however. Jody Kleinman remained adamant the city's answers made no sense and any information she received did little to dispel her fears or her criticism. "This is the same rhetoric over and over again, but the bottom line is, it's just not reasonable any longer to have a pumping oil well on the campus."

Many parents also questioned the legalities of a well on school grounds. Vice Mayor Mark Egerman addressed that issue, stating that no laws exist to govern an existing lease and there existed no grounds to force Venoco out. "Under current law, a new school cannot be built immediately adjacent to an oil production facility," Egerman explained. "At the time the Venoco site was developed, however, the law did not contain a minimum distance requirement between a new school and an oil production facility. Thus, the current Venoco operation is legal since it was lawful at the time the wells were drilled. An analogy would be a building that was built before more restrictive zoning was passed. The existing building would be a 'legally non-conforming use.' Similarly, the Venoco operation is a 'legally non-conforming use.'"

Parents asked the city to examine any potential legal rights to revoke the lease in light of the numerous Venoco violations. Kleinman was hopeful there was a way to eliminate the wells on legal grounds, but Egerman explained current law was written to allow companies with violations an opportunity to address problems. If the violation is corrected, the city or state has no legal justification to terminate. He acknowledged that various councilmembers had investigated this issue at length in hopes it might provide a method of closing the wells with a minimum of effort. Egerman admitted to me on a few occasions that closing the wells would have been preferable to the headaches it was causing the city.

Short of buying the Venoco operation out or refusing to renew their lease in 2016, any legal path appeared fruitless. One of the lawyers close to the case who wishes to remain anonymous confessed off the record that he had advised the council to act and eliminate future problems: "I suggested they buy out and close the wells, but I can tell you firsthand some officials disagreed it would be the best use of public monies."

Undeterred, Kleinman remained diligent in her efforts to rid the city of the wells. She hired experts and at her own expense (more than ten thousand dollars) gathered information to critique the city's testing results. "What I determined was needed was a cumulative health risk assessment encompassing all polluters in the area. It should be consistent with regulatory guidelines that set a standard of care to look at all sources with a potential to emit volatile organic compounds on our high-school campus. What the AQMD is asking Venoco to do, we need to do for our entire campus and at all of the sources.

"Second concerns the methane from a safety standpoint. I know it's a naturally occurring substance in the area, but they didn't sample adequately near or in the building. Los

Angeles has regulations for methane gas monitoring. Beverly Hills does not and although the city said they would put in methane monitors, how do we know until they do a complete scientific assessment and analysis where the monitors should be? Methane gas can be explosive."

Egerman attempted to assure Kleinman and others that the city shared the concern for any potential methane risk and was addressing the issue. "Methane measuring devices have alarms that are triggered when the methane reaches a certain level," he explained. "However, because methane and benzene are measured in parts per billion, we are looking into other types of devices to measure other hydrocarbons that would show when the levels reached measurements that would indicate further testing is necessary. We have asked CDM to develop this for us so we can do ongoing testing.

"The danger from methane comes when it seeps into a closed environment, such as a classroom, and has the potential to build up to dangerous levels. However, we found methane in the open field and if it did come to the surface, it would dissipate. We are asking CDM to examine whether venting is necessary and if it is, we will. We are relying on our experts and we will lean toward the side of caution." CDM was now fully involved in the testing and oversight of the wells, including the testing of soil gases on the field. Although the AQMD had agreed to follow up with its own testing, the city wanted to have results available to parents before the beginning of the new school year in 2003. Egerman pointed to the Grove shopping center in Los Angeles as an example of where methane monitoring was necessary because the potential for trapped gas was higher.

Despite reassurances about safety at the school many parents were not comforted, Mahshid Soleimani among them.

She explained her discomfort: "I believe that there were a few points brought up and when I asked what level of production Venoco was at when the tests were taken, no one said they had checked. They said they were told by Venoco they were in full production, but there was no proof or evidence of that. CDM couldn't even tell me Tuesday what the levels were when they took the tests."

Egerman countered her allegations. "CDM did check to determine the level of production during each time air samples were taken. CDM contacted Venoco to ascertain the level of gas and oil production at the time of each test. At the parents' meeting, a parent asked if the information given by Venoco was crosschecked with the written production records of Venoco. This check was not done by CDM, but will be done in the future."

This ongoing dialogue between parents and experts seemed to run in circles. Parents asked, city answered. Once the oil had escaped from Pandora's box, it was impossible to seal it again.

A discovery beneath the parking lot site of the proposed science and technology building presented new concerns and revitalized the discussion. "If you add the fact that some other company found an unknown oily substance under the parking lot north of building A when surveying for the Science and Tech building—and had to tell CDM to investigate this further—this concerns me greatly," Kleinman said. She pointed out that Dr. James LaVelle of CDM had said that when he was on the field, he himself had smelled the odors.

Soleimani, Kleinman, and other residents expressed concern over these noxious odors. "When the children are in an environment which is noxious, it is like being in a room full of smokers. It just isn't healthy or conducive to the learning atmosphere. Our children deserve better than that," Soleimani insisted.

She pointed to other issues that had not been explained to her satisfaction. "There were certain compounds present in the air when the oil well was operating and then lower when it wasn't. Why is this the case and why can't they explain this to us?"

District environmental consultant Mark Katchen of the Phylmar Group attempted an explanation for the varying chemical levels. "First of all, acetone [the active ingredient in nail polish remover] is also used as a paint thinner and sanitary cleaner. It can be manufactured, but acetone also occurs naturally and is biosynthesized in small amounts in the human body. MEK, methyl ethyl ketone or butanone, that dissolves many substances and is used as a solvent in processes involving gums, resins, cellulose acetate, and nitrocellulose coatings are not associated with petroleum production and are manufactured chemically, unless they are using them for cleanup.

"The other important thing is that the location of the MEK and acetone was crosswind of the oil well. This means that when doing sampling, wind blows onshore in the morning and offshore afternoons. So, standing on the upper field in the morning, the wind would be blowing at your face. In the afternoon it turns around and blows south toward your back. The acetone and MEK was crosswind or east of the well where the track loops around at the southeast corner. What this says is that if we picked up those MEK/acetone readings, it wasn't in the direct line or downwind of the oil well. Therefore, because acetone and MEK are not associated with oil production and they were crosswind, it doesn't appear the oil well is the source."

All testing and explanations aside, most parents agreed on the need for a comprehensive site risk assessment before they could be convinced of the safety of a pumping oil well on campus. Katchen endeavored to assure parents a health risk assessment would be included as part of CDM's subsurface evaluation.

Beverly Hills fine arts commissioner Hildy Hill voiced her discomfort with the lack of information about school safety. "I do think they should look at shutting it [the wells] down; at some point you have to say is it worth it." The belief that shutting down the wells was the best course of action was repeatedly expressed but never taken seriously enough to move on. Part of the reason for this lack of action was the financial aspect of buying a well and most importantly, the city was convinced, despite parents' objections, the well was safe.

Faced with the apparent reluctance to force Venoco off the high-school campus, parents persisted in examining the limited options to rid the city of the wells. One effort sought to place a referendum on the ballot requiring the Beverly Hills City Council to negotiate a deal with Venoco Inc. to purchase the site and cap the wells. The petition read,

> We the undersigned citizens of Beverly Hills, California hereby compel the City Council to negotiate a buyout for the oil wells property located at the Beverly Hills High School with the current owner, Venoco Inc.
>
> This negotiation will ultimately result in an amount of money to be paid to Venoco by the City of Beverly Hills which shall be raised and passed through a bond issue the amount of which shall be named in a second referendum passage of which must be predicated by a two-thirds vote by the city's citizens.
>
> I do hereby urge and compel the City Council of Beverly Hills to approach Venoco Inc. and negotiate an agreement for purchase in the name of the undersigned.

This presented a conundrum because it would have required

a bond be issued to fund the purchase. It was not a slam dunk all residents would necessarily sign on for that solution.

To the residents' chagrin, as each test returned within normal limits, the city's alternatives waned. "Good results limit our ability to find a legitimate legal reason to shut down the wells," Egerman told the parents. "If there were harmful levels we would have a leg to stand on legally. Although we are relieved to see levels within normal standards, it also poses a quandary for all of us who would like to eliminate the site."

In discussions about a referendum as a potential solution I became skeptical about the city's ability to even accomplish such a goal. Despite Soleimani's success at collecting the twenty-two hundred signatures necessary to force action, nothing was ever done by the city. Partly, I suspect it was the time required to legally check each signature's authenticity. This would have cost the city further. I don't believe there was a consensus among officials about the wisdom of closing the well before settling the case. It may have created an impression a problem existed—once again evidence that when lawyers become involved, the entire dynamic of the issue changes.

Most outsiders are surprised to learn that many residents in Beverly Hills receive royalties on slant oil drilling beneath the city. Despite public perception of resident wealth, the checks are usually a welcome perk. I was even told by one former city official that he would oppose any efforts to raise taxes on these royalties. However, I was assured by Mark Egerman that royalties played no part in any decision making process. Had the results been other than "normal amounts" at the well, safety would have remained the city's ultimate consideration. On a separate level, the responsibility for closing of the well would have fallen to the Division of Oil Gas and Geothermal Resources had there been egregious violations or health concerns.

Although test results had borne out a lack of evidence that emissions levels were unsafe, residents maintained the well was an unnecessary health and safety hazard, contributing to the already unhealthy air quality in the greater Los Angeles area. One study by the National Environmental Trust alleges that children in the Los Angeles Basin are exposed to more airborne pollutants by the age of twelve days than the EPA considers safe for a lifetime. The California Air Resources Board (CARB) reported that levels of the ten cancer-causing toxic air contaminants in the south coast region of the state— most notably, diesel exhaust particles—pose a cancer risk 1,005 times the EPA acceptable lifetime levels. CARB stated that the EPA's levels of acceptable exposure are calculated for the lifetime of an average adult and do not take into account the physiology of children and their increased outdoor exposure time.

In response, in March 2000, the AQMD launched an intensive one-year study to assess levels of cancer-causing toxic air pollutants and the risk they pose to Southland residents. "Since our last toxic air pollution study six years ago, we have reduced cancer-causing emissions through numerous regulations," Wallerstein told me. "This study will help us gauge the effectiveness of our current regulations and serve as a vital tool in helping shape future air quality and environmental justice."

The AQMD began collecting air samples for some substances in the Multiple Air Toxics Exposure Study III (MATES III) with a goal toward updating toxic air pollution levels and toxic emissions inventories. The data was then used to produce a computer model of air dispersion to determine the cancer, as well as non-cancer, risks from air toxins across Southern California. The study also investigated potential toxic hot spots in communities. Employing moveable monitoring stations, they sampled a dozen or more neighborhood sites near toxic emissions sources or in areas where community members were concerned about health risks from air pollution. This included neighborhoods near airports, railroads, warehouses, landfills, high-volume vehicle traffic, or multiple commercial or industrial facilities.

But the air quality at schools had not gone unnoticed in Beverly Hills or elsewhere in California. Sen. Martha Escutia, a Democrat from Norwalk, coauthored SB 352 in 2003. "More and more children are breathing dirty air because they go to schools right next to our busiest freeways," Escutia explained at the time. "SB 352 will allow California's children to concentrate on learning, rather than breathing." The measure required new schools to be set back from freeways and other busy roads by at least five hundred feet, unless the school took steps to improve air quality to a point that it posed no threat to student health. Escutia cited a study by the California Environmental Protection Agency showing that pollution levels are as much as 25 times higher near freeways than at sites set back from busy transportation corridors. According to Escutia, these regulations would essentially force both existing and new school sites to follow the same standards. The mitigation for the new requirements would be locally controlled by the school boards and elected officials in the area.

She continued, "My big focus is schools, especially since there are so many schools in my district located in industrial areas. There was arsenic on a playground and one junior high school is next to a chrome plating plant. I'm a mother and it's scary." She admitted it was understandably difficult for districts to site new schools; however, she believes that science is still evolving and people need more test results to become more informed. "So many districts are in desperate need of space for schools. Where do you site a school, on an earthquake fault or a methane field and cap it. You take a risk in everything when there is new construction. It's a pick your poison situation." Nevertheless, she states, "No school board in their right mind would site a school on top of an environmental hazard today."

Gennet Paauwe, a spokesman for the California Air Resources Board, told me new standards for particulates were being adopted as a result of Escutia's bill. I had called her to consult her about Beverly Hills' plight. "We are always sensitive near children. The local sources like AQMD have purview and we haven't seen any problem. We do the audits and from what we've seen everything is on the up and up. All the agencies are working together to reduce emissions, including the ships coming in to the Los Angeles port."

Emissions levels at the port are egregious and contribute heavily to the pollution in the area. Paauwe said simply slowing down the ships' speed as they enter the port cuts down on emissions of particulate matter. "We are working to cut emissions, but these are international ships and we can't force them. If we make it too difficult it may be cheaper to use another port and have the goods trucked or trained down, which would add to pollution. But we are working with the parties involved, including the shippers, and so far they are cooperating. You hope the parties have the best interests of everyone at heart and have to give people a chance to do the right thing and this effort has been fairly recent."

In the years since, the state has implemented new restrictions on the ports with the implementation of the Clean Truck Program. Although its intention was to eliminate dangerously high-polluting trucks from the Long Beach port area, it was also met with challenges from various groups that insisted it would harm minorities who could not afford better trucks and bankrupt fleet owners. This is the perfect example of why it is so difficult to clean up America's air. When pollution becomes a political issue for some, it delays the process for all.

Such cases were only part of the new language spoken in Beverly Hills. In addition to writing about a Beverly Hills matron's birthday luncheon at the Peninsula Hotel, I was suddenly reporting on test results showing:

- Diesel exhaust is responsible for about 70 percent of the total cancer risk from air pollution;
- Emissions from mobile sources—including cars and trucks as well as ships, trains, and planes—account for about 90 percent of the cancer risk. Emissions from businesses and industry are responsible for the remaining 10 percent; and
- The highest cancer risk is found in south Los Angeles County—including the port area—and along major freeways. Although testing is done, standards are reexamined and raised, the oil well at the school could not be proven to be a health hazard or contribute excessively to air quality in the area.

On the menu along with Nate 'n Al's corned beef were butadiene, manganese, acetaldehyde, methylene chloride, arsenic, naphthalene, benzene, chloroform, formaldehyde, hexavalent chromium, and a laundry list of noxious chemicals. Many who had previously spent their time addressing mundane daily issues confronting the city were now able to name toxic chemicals as easily as the latest Fendi bag. The new vocabulary proved unsettling to some and contributed to the fears of many. To a layman, it is difficult to make sense of this jargon, as experts speak in parts per million, parts per billion, VOC levels, or an alphabet soup of confusing toxic chemicals.

Most residents admitted they would be less afraid had they any notion what these "experts" were talking about and I concurred. Although many seemed content to receive information from council and school board meetings, the newspaper, or calling various sources like the Air Quality Management District and the Department of Oil, Gas and Geothermal Resources, there was a group of parents who insisted on an even freer flow of information. To appease the appetite of these residents, the City Council initiated a parents' group and met with them at intervals throughout the testing process.

Press was not allowed into these meetings, so I had to obtain information secondhand, not something I am fond of doing and I complained bitterly to no avail. At least I was fortunate enough to have a reliable source. My "guy on the inside" was Jody Kleinman and I trusted her reports and comments. Kleinman remembers most of these meetings as a rehash of the newest test results while parents lashed out at the city, demanding more be done to ensure site safety. They were adamant that soil testing should be done to ensure that no toxins had leeched into the ground water or soil where the children ran and played each day.

Although the city's policy was to allow access to the meetings, some parents, such as Ari Bussel, who possesses an email doumenting the refused access, were denied on the grounds that the council was limiting the number to parents previously selected. Mayor Tom Levyn, whom Bussel had emailed requesting to be put on the list, could not remember rejecting Ari: "I do recall we had parent and community meetings. We tried to have small group meetings so that everyone present could ask questions. We never intended to restrict anyone's access to information."

On that subject, Jody Kleinman says, "Initially, we had asked the city and AQMD for public town hall meetings, open to everyone, but that never happened. If you have nothing to hide, why hide anything?" She does admit, however, to understanding the city's hesitancy in gathering hundreds of highly charged residents together to point loud, emotional fingers.

I asked about the space limitations and was told for the sake of space and efficiency it was necessary to keep the attendees to a "reasonable" level. Mark Egerman disputes any restrictions, explaining, "Any parent who wished to attend a meeting could come. We tried to keep the meetings at no more than around twenty people. So, if thirty parents requested to be present, we would hold two meetings of fifteen each." Occasionally these contradictory responses would occur amongst officials, but 99 percent of the time everyone appeared to be in accord.

The group of parents eventually split into the naysayers and those who believed the well was safe. Only three or four meetings were held and one was an opportunity to meet with a CDM representative and discuss test results.

Meanwhile, Jody Kleinman continued to show up at council meetings in an attempt to convince the city to close the well down. "Every new piece of information that is revealed convinces me there is absolutely no upside to having the oil wells near our children. We have to take steps to protect the students of Beverly and nearby residents from any potential problems."

Legally the city's hands were tied. Since the wells had existed on the field before the school was established, the city had few options. Egerman explained the only legal way to close the wells would be if a health hazard was proven. Since the tests had thus far come back within "normal" limits for Los Angeles air quality, the city had no choice. As long as the air surrounding the site complied with state VOC standards nothing could be done. Their only option would be a refusal to release the property to the oil company when their current lease expired in 2016.

Nevertheless, a new potential battlefront was opened when some Beverly Hills citizens discovered a section of the municipal code restricting city oil production. Optimistic they had stumbled upon a magic bullet to aid in closing the site, parents—led by Janet Morris, Mahshid Soleimani, and Jody Kleinman—urged the school board to consider municipal code Article 3, Oil Wells, Sec. 10-5.306, which states:

> (c) The Council finds and determines that the location of drill sites on real property within the City, other than on the real property described in this section [the Venoco site], designated as a controlled drill site, would be contrary to the best interests of the citizens and residents of the City and the public health, safety, and general welfare of the citizens and inhabitants of the City. Drilling from or on the subsurface of real property within the City, except from or upon a controlled drill site described in this section, is hereby prohibited, and the drilling of an oil and gas or oil or gas well from any drilling site in the City, except from or on a controlled drill site described in this section, shall constitute a public nuisance and shall be abated as provided in Section 10-5.322 of this Article.

Janet Morris urged consideration of the municipal code as an option for Venoco's closure and cited the two thousand signatories of the petition previously presented to the board.

According to Morris, an oil production facility on school grounds is an inappropriate use of school property. "I question why the council deems it proper to allow oil production at the school and considers it a health risk in other areas of the city. The ordinance gives the city the right to revoke Venoco's permit for persistent violation of any laws by the permitee. There is clear evidence that Venoco has vented illegally on numerous occasions . . . a clear violation of the law."

Beverly Hills officials believed the city should further examine the parents' charges to ensure that was truly the case, but to no avail.

"Anxious, concerned and sometime angry parents added their names to this petition to reach our elected officials," Soleimani said. "I am aware that the school district expected the enrollment at the school to be one hundred less than it was last year. Obviously, some parents chose to leave. This petition is the voice of parents who chose to stay and fight for Beverly Hills High School. We say BHHS should stand for 'Better, Healthier, Happier, and Safer.'"

The constant discourse continued with no respite and it seemed inevitable Giorgio perfume wasn't destined to be the only prevalent scent on Rodeo Drive.

5

History Repeats Itself

History repeats itself, first as tragedy, second as farce.

—Karl Marx

Masry and his team were relentless in their investigation into the wells. They appeared determined to ensure no stone in the list of possible allegations be left unturned. Although Beverly Hills had little history of environmental issues, an incident from 1999 resurfaced during the early lawsuit years, bringing new allegations from the Masry/Brockovich camp. Masry accused the Board of Education of whitewashing the results of a 1999 environmental study concerning air quality at both the high school and Beverly Vista Elementary School portable classrooms. "Our experts analyzed the results and we think the person reading the report either didn't understand or there was a deliberate cover-up," Masry told me.

Remembering this "cover-up" strategy had proven successful against PG&E, I looked for information to discern if a case could be made that the city had hidden the air quality dangers in the portables years earlier. Masry & Vititoe's Jim Drury claimed the board had failed to let the parents and community know tests were taken that had uncovered a problem, but then-school-board president Barry Brucker recalled the incident and how the board dealt with the issue. He also noted how similar local CBS broadcast coverage of the oil wells was to their portable buildings sweeps week story, leading with the headline, "Cancer in Beverly Hills Schools." He stated, "We did end up getting an apology follow-up story from CBS News whereby they stated that our school district was a model for all school districts to follow regarding health and safety for their students. Call it coincidence, but Drew Griffin was the reporter on both stories."

Brucker explained that when the school board decided to close down Beverly Vista Elementary following damage from the Northridge earthquake, they purchased or rented new portable buildings. "The company who provided them [the largest in Southern California] had used a formaldehyde-based glue for the carpeting. The off-gassing from the glue was causing headaches in some of the kids and staff. When we discovered all of this we upped the air exchanges on the air conditioning to move the air in and out more often and this seemed to eliminate the problem." They also changed the carpeting, but Brucker said this did not satisfy some parents who "freaked out and one parent moved their kid out of the school.

"We spent a fortune on testing and educating," he said and disputed allegations of any cover-up of the problem, insisting the community was not only kept apprised of the results and testing, it was done at their behest. "We formed a parent/citizens/staff committee to oversee the testing and we sent letters to all the community to tell them what was happening. I also sent mass e-mails in my CUB [Community Updates Bulletin] report issuing updates."

In Brucker's July-September CUB report, the following was announced:

Bungalows/Indoor Air Quality: In June, an article was written in the *L.A. Times* and *The Wall Street Journal* about alleged poor indoor air quality in portable classrooms which rattled not only our community, but the nation.

This nationwide concern focused on high-profile Beverly Vista School as CBS-TV ran a tabloid feature in front of that campus. I am very proud of our District's response by contracting with testing labs, hiring an indoor air quality consultant, holding town forums to hear the community's concerns and forming an Environmental Safety Committee (ESC).

The ESC is comprised of staff, parents, physicians, administrators and community volunteers. They are charged with making recommendations to the Board and evaluating, analyzing and recommending appropriate remediation measures.

With only two short months before school was to reopen, our staff worked around the clock to remediate our bungalows on all campuses to standards that met or exceeded all known guidelines. The end result of this collective effort resulted in a successful opening of school and CBS News doing a follow-up report stating that BHUSD is the model school district for indoor air quality advocacy. Thank you to our exceptional staff and our Environmental Safety Committee parents in the district.

At that time, a letter was also sent out to the community from then-superintendent Richard Bertain notifying parents that all testing results were available for review in the Environmental Document Repository at the district office. It read, in part, "In the meantime we have begun a comprehensive maintenance program, starting at Beverly Vista. As these modifications are complete we will retest the air quality in each classroom to ensure a healthful and safe environment for our students and teachers. We will not allow occupation of an unhealthy classroom. Updated information will be available at the district's website and follow-up letters in the near future."

Brucker recalled that during the portable classroom incident, some "radical" parents had located a toxicologist. Their "expert" came to the school board forum on the subject with a group of parents from Simi Valley. "He arrived in scrubs with volumes of books and was a complete fraud. Through our consultant we recruited the top environmental hazard air quality person, a doctor and professor from UCLA, who came in a business suit and wiped the other doctor off the floor with facts. In fact, the other doctor brought books that were written by our consultant. Apparently, the fraud toxicologist was looking for business by doing major testing on our kids and saw dollar signs." Relating the incident to me, Brucker laughed when reminded that "some of our brightest parents like Hildy Hill cold-cocked the fraud MD with questions, and he fell flat on his face."

Since I had not been at the *Beverly Hills Courier* when the bungalows were investigated and therefore not privy to the facts firsthand, I searched through old articles and spoke to parents who had been directly involved. *Courier* reporters Ben Davidson and Imee Gacad both covered the issue and wrote in-depth pieces on the controversy.

Former Beverly Hills parent Lorraine Mestman disagrees with the statement that the city did all they could to fix the problem. She pulled her children out of Beverly Hills schools and sent them to private ones over the issue. Mestman was unsatisfied with the city's response and believed they refused to take further precautions because of financial considerations. "When I asked why they weren't making certain changes to mitigate the problem, they responded it was too expensive to fix."

To satisfy her own environmental curiosity about the wells, she attended the Brockovich/Masry meeting at the Beverly Hills Hotel although her children had already left the district. "I believed and still do that there is a problem. I was also surprised to see the way some residents reacted to the issue. After the meeting the woman next to me turned and whispered, 'I hope this isn't true or our property values will drop to nothing.'"

Another parent I interviewed about the portables was Linda Roberts. She is not one to mince words and vocally criticized the district on those occasions she believed they were acting in opposition to the children's best interests. Unafraid, she has always spoken her mind in the severest of terms concerning their decisions. Certain she would not defend any misdeeds by the board, I asked if they had acted appropriately. Her assessment of the school board's behavior was favorable. Roberts, whose husband Mike served as a Recreation and Parks commissioner, stated that the district was completely forthcoming with parents and the community at that time. Responding to Masry's allegations of a cover-up, Roberts said, "That's not true. As a grandparent and active community member at Beverly Hills High School, I was aware that once the district found out there may be an air problem, they went out immediately and changed the carpeting.

"This was no secret, they jumped on it instantly and took care of everything in a timely manner. Then they tested numerous times as a follow-up after everything was okay. There was no cover-up; all the parents knew about this as it was happening. We were informed instantly and the entire community knew."

In an article from August 1999, reporter Davidson addressed the issue of toxins in the bungalows' carpeting, writing,

According to Jack Volner, account manager for Collins and Aikman [who had supplied the carpet to the schools], the uniqueness of the carpeting can be attributed to the fact that its backing is a vinyl composite closed cell which doesn't breathe and is impermeable to air and moisture, like a vinyl roof system.

According to Volner, with the new carpet in place, VOCs [volatile organic compounds] will no longer be able to come up through the floor in significant amounts and enter the air flow. This, in concert with improved ventilation systems currently being installed in the bungalows, as well as other modifications in equipment and maintenance, are hoped to reduce the VOCs to far below standard levels.

A report issued by Mark Katchen from the Phylmar Group noted that once the changes were made and tests conducted under the optimum conditions, the results returned to safe levels. Katchen wrote, "The estimated incremental cancer risks associated with the levels of chemicals detected in the 45 different re-locatable units during the August, September, and October sampling at Beverly Vista Elementary and Beverly Hills High School are all very consistent. In summary, the risks associated with the incremental concentrations of chemicals at each individual re-locatable unit are below the target level that is used by certain regulatory programs as the basis for requiring some form of action."

Despite being presented with the facts of the incident, Masry continued to disagree with the city's conclusions and argued that the school whitewashed the problem in the portables. "Our experts analyzed the results and either there was a cover-up or the person who did the report didn't know what they were doing. It was one or the other.

"We found levels 5,200 percent over the action of safety

levels on benzene and 40,000 times over the action levels of safety of formaldehyde. There were other chemicals, but these were the two most troubling."

He criticized the board for not removing the children from the classrooms, failing to notify any government entity, and simply increasing the air conditioners. "You have a situation where you have four hundred times over safety levels and you're going to increase the air conditioning. That was their solution and that to me is pathetic.

"What's interesting is that two testing companies do this and the lab that did it was the same as we use."

Referencing his new lawsuit, Masry insisted they were "totally confident" the emissions coming out of the ground as well as the radioactive radon gas and iodine 131 being injected into the wells to bring the oil up could cause Hodgkin's Disease and thyroid cancer. "I'm not remotely concerned that we can't prove it was caused by the oil well at BHHS." He contended, "Although the wells may be safe at this moment, once the temperature rises to 75 degrees and the ground is dry, the emissions level will rise again."

Katchen disputed their theory and pointed out that state tests of radon by zip code show the levels at the high school to be zero. Mike Edwards, vice president of Venoco, responded to the iodine allegations, explaining injections are done once a year, as required by the Division of Oil, Gas and Geothermal Resources. "This ensures the wells are operating properly and the levels [of iodine] are low and diluted continually. It is placed into the earth at eight thousand feet below the surface and cannot escape into the environment."

Masry remained consistent in his opinion and criticism of the AQMD, saying, "I have no quarrel with the AQMD except that it took them thirty years to get out there. I think right now the school is probably safe. If the wells are fully operational and the temperature reaches 75 or above, I wouldn't send my kid to that school."

Noting the irony of being school board president during both environmental events, Brucker waxed philosophical over his fortunes. "I was glad to be in a position of leadership to tackle the challenges that came upon us in both of these instances, although I do have a few more grey hairs because of it. God only puts you in positions that you can handle.

"In one case we had a real student health concern with the portables, in the other case we were battling a plaintiff that was courting a movie deal. Both possessed terrific challenges, one that involved science and remediation and the other that involved tabloid reporters, ambulance-chasing lawyers, and movie deals for Brockovich."

Notwithstanding varying legal opinions, test results continued to return within standard levels. Dr. Barry Wallerstein, executive director of the AQMD, said he would soon issue a report on air quality findings and make it available to everyone.

Superintendent Dr. Gwen Gross issued a statement assuring parents that tests results continued to be favorable.

> Since our last meeting, the AQMD conducted more air sampling on April 19th at five locations: three locations within Beverly Hills High School, the property of Venoco, and nearby Roxbury Park. These results were consistent with those reported by AQMD in February and earlier in April. Again, the AQMD has reported that test results continue to be "well below" the health limits established by the State of California.
>
> During Spring Break, the City's environmental engineering consultant—Camp, Dresser, McKee (CDM)—conducted a series of air tests at the high school. An executive summary of preliminary

findings is expected within the next ten days. That will be made public. A full report, including backup data, will then be prepared and should be available several weeks later. That document will also be made available to parents and the public.

Jim Drury questioned the city's testing methods. "If they are doing soil gas testing, are they installing soil gas monitors [which should be used]? There should be a risk assessment done at the school. LAUSD [Los Angeles Unified School District] does a risk assessment every time they build a new school to make sure the site is safe. Why shouldn't Beverly Hills have the same kinds of safeguards?"

Mark Katchen disagreed with Drury. "The methodology is standard. A soil gas sample is relatively static and nonchanging except over longer or intermittent periods of time. What we're trying to do here is access what's down there. We could install wells or monitors, but for an initial evaluation this is standard procedure. Why would you put in long-term monitoring devices if there is nothing there to monitor? We might find something and then we would make a decision, but initially we're just trying to see if something's there."

In determining any potential health threat, he said they are concerned with chronic hazard effects from the site. "If in fact there is only a problem once in a while, we have to factor that into the risk assessment. Obviously, the risk factor is less because the exposure isn't there. If we have so much data and it takes that much to establish an excessive background level, it obviously means it doesn't happen that often and it's an infrequent occurrence. That means the exposure and therefore the risk is significantly less."

Katchen believed the testing performed was extensive. "If they said they [Brockovich and Masry] found a problem after only two samples and we have more than sixty sample events already, you would think if they found a problem, we would have a better chance of finding it if it was there. You would think we would have picked it up by now." Katchen was adamant that testing would continue until the city was satisfied there was no reason to persist. "We're not going to stop testing until we're satisfied there's no risk. At the present time we don't see any risk at all above background levels, but we will keep testing."

The city opined that substantiating Masry's numbers was made more difficult because he had only furnished a small portion of his data, which lacked facts establishing where sampling was conducted. Masry was upset by the city's attitude: "The city acts like I'm out there for myself. All I'm doing is responding to an inquiry from concerned people who are getting sick and dropping dead from cancer at a young age. I went out and did preliminary sampling and I would do a danger risk assessment if they would let me on campus."

Although I repeatedly asked Masry and his team for proof of their claims, I was waved off and told, "You'll see everything when we get to court." Masry informed me there was much data to review and, "No, it was not unusual for it to take this long in these situations." I continually asked why, if they possessed a smoking gun, they refused to share the information, especially if children's health was at issue and the very problem they were there to address. No one ever answered my query, save with assertions that they gave the city everything and the truth would come out in court.

This claim ultimately opened another battlefront in an already fully raging war. The city vehemently disputed Masry's contention that he provided all testing information. This gap left the city in a quandary: the veracity of Erin Brockovich's allegations concerning the chemical levels of her original testing. Test results were crucial to the plaintiffs' case, but the city was puzzled about why numbers varied so greatly between Erin's test levels and the AQMD's. Brockovich's exact testing locations were unknown and necessary to ensure appropriate test areas were addressed. Since the city and school district were not satisfied they had been presented with all the necessary papers concerning Erin's results, they were forced to employ uncommon methods to secure the information.

City Attorney Larry Wiener attempted numerous times to procure the documents to no avail. It was apparent to Wiener the answers would not be readily forthcoming, so he laid out the council options as a last-ditch effort to acquire the information. One avenue open was the council's power to invoke a legislative subpoena. Beverly Hills had never before in its history found this option necessary. Skip Miller, one of the city's attorneys, proposed that the council exercise that alternative and it was instantly adopted.

The city council came out swinging on June 3, 2003, evoked their legislative powers, and issued subpoenas to parties involved in the dispute. They voted unanimously to "establish a legislative proceeding to investigate the allegations of health risks from the oil wells at Beverly Hills High School, authorize the City Council to issue subpoenas pursuant to Government Code Section 37104, and approved the issuance of subpoenas to obtain information pertinent to the subject matter of the City Council's investigation." The subpoena was filed in Los Angeles Superior Court in July of that year.

Wiener said the council's move established a fact-finding process to aid in important decisions. He was adamant and issued a statement that they would continue their attempts to unearth any yet undisclosed facts and compare the results firsthand: "We are committed to doing whatever it takes to ensure that we know the truth about the safety of environmental conditions at the high school. We would hope Masry would also share that interest and provide the information we are seeking. If they fail to comply they would be in contempt of court."

The mandate compelled production of information pertinent to the investigation. This included forcing Masry & Vititoe as well as Baron and Budd, the law firm partnering with Ed Masry's firm, to present all findings and protocol for their original testing. The legislative subpoena left Masry no option but to finally comply with the city's requests to deliver his testing documents for examination. At least so the council thought.

Masry's testing guru Jim Drury declared he was shocked by the subpoena. "Why is the city so scared of us? We haven't even filed yet." Responding to Drury's surprise, Wiener explained that the council was "merely addressing some seeming contradictions in the data that demanded more information about plaintiffs' data and testing protocol."

Despite the city's extreme action, Masry continued to insist he gave the city what was required and it was they who were not forthcoming with their testing. Wiener vehemently contradicted that accusation, adding that the city's numbers and data were made public numerous times and remained available to everyone on the school district's website. He explained that Masry had only furnished a partial portion of his data, lacking in certain facts that would have established where the sampling was conducted.

The city's experts had problems with Masry's graph showing a spike in benzene numbers without furnishing location or follow-up data. On Masry's graph, the November 16, 2002, test showed a reading of non-detect. On November

17, 2002, the reading level was at nine parts per billion for benzene but furnished no location. On December 8, 2002, the graph showed a level of 1.8 for benzene, with no location noted. The background sample of that same day, which is almost two parts per billion, also provided no location. On the January 5 sampling by the Masry firm, there was a non-detect reading on the benzene levels. Other numbers on the charts fell within the same ranges of the data taken by the AQMD and CDM (Camp, Dresser & McKee) tests.

One apparent contradiction was evident in spiked levels of eighteen parts per billion of benzene after a grab sampling by Masry's team on January 5, but on that same day there is a sampling of an eight-hour Summa canister by Masry's team and the results show non-detect. This posed a conundrum for the city, not only because one level measured abnormally high against the standard background levels but also because a non-detect reading had been recorded on the same day. Such diverse testing numbers, coupled with a lack of exact locations and protocol, ultimately forced the city's hand.

When asked how the contradiction in the test results was possible, Columbia Analytical Services director of Research and Development Mike Tuday, also subpoenaed, commented, "It would be possible to get that diversity of results; however, it is unusual in an outdoor sampling to have an absolute non-detect for an eight-hour time-integrated sample."

AQMD executive director Dr. Barry Wallerstein, himself a graduate of BHHS, took a personal interest in the events. During our conversations, Dr. Wallerstein noted chain of custody as an important sampling issue. To guarantee no one could question their results, AQMD staff stood by the canisters for the entire eight hours to ensure no tampering and that readings were accurate. I accompanied them on their first round of testing to witness the process firsthand and take photographs for the paper.

"Chain of custody may also provide an explanation for whether or not the Masry canisters may have been inadvertently contaminated," Wallerstein proffered. "It may explain why there is such a discrepancy and the high levels of acetone and MEK [a chemical harmful if inhaled or absorbed through skin that affects the central nervous system and causes irritation to skin, eyes, and respiratory tract], two pollutants not usually found in high numbers in oil emissions."

Wallerstein's comments sparked my curiosity and I decided to examine the chain of custody issue in depth with someone with whom I shared a privileged conversation. It was beneficial to have my own scientific "Deep Throat," for as I quickly learned, where huge sums of money and controversial lawsuits are involved, experts are not always willing to go on the record. I felt fortunate to find someone close to the situation who agreed to speak anonymously and impartially about the facts. It helped me gain a bit more perspective and objectivity about the issues.

When I first learned about Erin's allegations I had no reason to believe they were not valid. After all, like so many others who had seen the movie with Julia Roberts, I accepted her as the crusader of environmental issues, the duly designated and legally anointed "Green Queen." My first conversation with her hexavalent chromium highness further convinced me of her sincerity. She assured me the benzene levels at her testing site were higher than the 405 Freeway at rush hour. All Californians are aware that this toxic freeway air, if harnessed, could be used in chemical warfare. I had no reason to doubt her veracity and admittedly, I did not. That first discourse with Erin ignited my determination to be an advocate and watchdog for the community. I had returned to my true believer roots and began channeling Abbie Hoffman, minus the drugs, heavy on the chocolate.

A story of this magnitude was ions above the usual benign blather covered in a Beverly Hills community paper, and as a child of the 1960s, I was chomping at the bit to sink my teeth into something of substance. So passionate was I about the accusations, Mayor MeraLee Goldman doubted I could be objective enough to cover the story and warned school board president Barry Brucker and superintendent Gwen Gross against allowing me access. Thankfully, they decided to ignore her advice and had faith I could report the story credibly, despite the outcome or my personal feelings. Brucker and Dr. Gross also believed if the facts proved the site safe, the community would be more inclined to believe what I wrote because, as they noted, "I had earned and possessed the community's trust."

When I met with former mayor and then-councilman Mark Egerman, I told him I would report whatever the testing showed, be it bad or good, and actively resist any attempt to censor information. To Egerman's credit, he assured me there would be no interference. I do believe the council attempted to live up to this promise to the best of their ability. I am also aware there is a certain amount of secrecy inherent in public policy, especially when litigation has reared its costly head. To this day I believe the city was forthcoming probably 95 percent of the time.

Enlisting my scientific Deep Throat was a most informative and lucky break for a science novice. During our first conversation, I sought answers to two questions: were Erin's results probable and was there evidence of chain of custody for her testing?

Understanding the nature of the claims was beneficial. Excess levels of benzene and other volatile organic compounds are regulated on the basis of ultimate health impacts to the population. A certain amount of toxic chemicals are always present in the air, allowed if within the bounds of what has been deemed an acceptable risk. If there is a rise in the levels of toxins where a polluter is present, it is obvious the increase is a result of that nearby facility.

Excess amounts are harmful to health with potential to corrupt human immune systems and instigate the onset of various diseases. Over the years these levels have changed as new knowledge and testing challenged the safety of certain previously accepted toxin levels. Many chemicals once used freely and considered safe were later banned as new information and testing adjusted the standards. One such chemical in the Beverly Hills toxic cocktail is chromium six, an anticorrosive and proven carcinogen now banned for certain uses since the early 1990s.

The impact of these airborne toxins is predicated on many components. Among these, the amount and duration of the exposure and proximity to the chemical before it is inhaled. Factors including age, genetic disposition and additional environmental contributions create risk. Much like alcohol, the more you are exposed, the more the body absorbs and the greater the affect. Also like alcohol, each person possesses a certain amount of resistance that varies with the individual; however, chemicals are regulated with a variety of exposure factors in mind.

Additional specifics about the derrick may help clarify the oil well's emission of toxins. VOCs are emitted through the top of the derrick, 165 feet above ground. They enter the air, drop, and are disseminated to some extent as they fall. Fugitive emissions closer to ground level are released from the valves or any leaks in the system.

To address the variables, testing was done at numerous sites surrounding the high school and also at various heights. The bleachers adjacent to the soccer field were checked due to their close proximity to the Sempra Energy facility. Levels were measured underground at the base of the wells as well as ground level at Venoco's site.

It should be noted that less attention was paid to the Sempra facility because it is in Century City and completely enclosed. However, I possess pictures of the Sempra site taken in the 1970s showing clouds of steam expelled into the air. The steam contained a toxic cocktail of various chemicals including formaldehyde, chromium six, and various carcinogens. Today this mix of chemicals would be inspected and addressed, yet it was ignored in the past when the government was more cavalier about air issues.

In my first conversation with my scientific source, when I inquired about Erin's discovery of high concentrations of benzene emissions at a level "somewhere near the bleachers," my expert pointed out an important consideration. He explained that due to the oil well's height, emissions spewing from atop the wells would, like rain, be somewhat dispersed before landing at various points on the ground below. As the chemicals were scattered they would lose concentration and upon landing would exhibit lower toxic levels.

"So would it be possible to secure such high levels of toxins as Erin alleges after landing on the ground?" I asked.

"No, probably not."

"Then how would you get such high numbers?"

"The only way to achieve those results would be to hold the Summa canister [the oval metal container used to capture and measure the air] at the very opening of the well as it exits the stack over 165 feet in the air, or get them from somewhere else."

"Where?"

"Anywhere there might be a smaller space with high concentrations of emissions."

"Do you know if this is the case?"

"That's the problem. It's impossible to know because there was no chain of custody."

"Chain of custody?" I asked.

"If Erin took the tests, and no witnesses were present, the tech who reads the results at the laboratory has no way of knowing from where they were acquired. One can only read and report on the levels, not vouch for where or how they were obtained. There could also be a possibility of contamination before they reached the lab."

"So the lab reports can't be fully validated if no chain of custody exists?"

"Exactly. Those results may be high, but where they were collected, no lab tech can ever avow."

That is the gist of my conversation with my anonymous scientific expert. From that time forward, I was skeptical. Without valid testing of all these areas of dispute, no definitive conclusions about safety or health could truly be discerned.

6

Frustration Builds

One man's transparency is another's humiliation.
— Gerry Adams

Community members who attended one parents' meeting were told the city had temporarily suspended testing. At that meeting, parents were furnished with the complete data from the CDM testing and the results of the indoor air sampling at the high school by Mark Katchen. However, some at the meeting were frustrated and angry over delays in further testing that included the soil gases portion of the process. "When we get an answer to the subpoenas we will analyze whether there is other information to lead us to believe we should alter the testing program," Wiener explained.

Jody Kleinman was among the disgruntled parents. "They hand-selected us to be the spokespeople and we went along with it because they promised we would get scientific data and a risk assessment. Now they tell us we have to wait for Masry's results."

Brucker assured Kleinman that although the tests were put on hold, all data thus far collected had shown no reason for concern. "So far, there has been no credible data to support further testing. Up until now, every test taken has shown no significant levels of toxic chemicals present. However, the community needs to know that there is basic information missing from Masry's reports which would explain apparent contradictions in his sampling results."

Comments of PTA council president Myra Lurie, later elected to the school board, reflected the consensus of parents regarding delays in disseminating information about campus safety. "This issue has taken on a life of its own, aside from the legalities. I think the city needs to be open with the parents and provide all the testing necessary to allay their fears. Although all the testing thus far has been reassuring, the community needs to know that the city is doing all it can scientifically and it will share its findings."

Katchen pointed out the importance of having all the data to focus further testing. "I understand the parents' concerns, but without the missing information we are unable to ensure that we are doing the appropriate tests," he explained.

In seeking that data, the city issued subpoenas to Bernard Endres, the toxicologist hired by the Masry & Vititoe law firm; the custodian of records from Sempra Energy, which operates a heating and cooling facility adjacent to the high school; Baron and Budd law firm in Dallas, Texas, the litigators contracted by Masry to try the case; Masry & Vititoe; Venoco, Inc.; Columbia Analytical Services, the facility that read the test results for Masry's firm; and Zymax Forensics in San Luis Obispo, who had also participated in reading the test results. However, this tactic did not settle anything. The sparring continued until the information was ultimately wrangled away in court.

The saga resumed when attorneys squared off in court and the city requested a contempt citation against Erin

Brockovich and Ed Masry for failure to comply with the legislative subpoena. In another surprising turn, plaintiff lawyers admitted in open court that they had not conducted epidemiological studies to justify claims of cancer excesses caused by oil emissions at the high school. Although the city believed this admission to be a coup, Erin and her lawyers seemed to take it all in stride.

Skip Miller, attorney for the City of Beverly Hills, informed Los Angeles Superior Court judge Valerie Baker that Brockovich had made statements in the press alleging facts and figures and claiming to have scientific evidence to support her data. "Yet in truth they have failed to provide any proof to the city after so ordered by the court," he said.

Brockovich and Masry's attorneys, Al Stewart and Rick Ottaiano, claimed her statements were misunderstood. They told Judge Baker that Brockovich had checked the national cancer statistics to garner figures but had never conducted any studies of her own. Judge Baker agreed to take the issue under advisement, but city attorneys agreed this seemingly small statement carried a great deal of weight. Miller was certain it would cast doubt on the veracity of Brockovich's statements about well safety and her emissions claims. Wiener, too, believed the admission was significant: "When put to the test in court, they were forced to admit that they have no evidence to support their claims."

Epidemiology played an important role in the allegations at the heart of the lawsuit. Many parents insisted the safety of the site could not be proven conclusively until a full study was concluded. As I came to understand, the term had relevance, but what is entailed in conducting a complete epidemiological study? How could it benefit either side and what are the limitations?

An epidemiological study is a statistical study attempting to link human health effects to a specific cause. It has been an accepted method of public health research and is used in evidence-based medicine to identify risk factors for disease and determine optimal treatment approaches to clinical practice. In Beverly Hills' case, its use in the study of communicable and non-communicable diseases, including outbreak investigation design study, data collection, and analysis, would be important. Scientists also rely on biology, geographic information science to store data and map disease patterns, and social science disciplines to understand risk factors. In layman's terms it is a protocol for determining disease, risks, and contributing factors.

How does such a study relate to cancer allegations and why was the admission of a lack of such a study important in the courtroom? Erin and the attorneys spoke a great deal about the "excess" of cancers at the high school. They claimed this profusion was evidence a problem existed and therefore a direct link could be drawn between the oil well and student illness. This was a foundation for their lawsuit and therefore a highly important component of the case. If there were no excess of cancers in the student population, it would be difficult to prove the rates of illnesses were nothing more than the average rates of occurrence one could expect to find in the general population.

The caveat was that no significant epidemiological study could be concluded in a matter of weeks or months. There are a great many variables involved in this or any case. For example, the years covered in the lawsuit spanned three decades. To locate such a high number of students would be expensive and time consuming, if possible at all. It was not only students who were involved. There were residents, visitors to the city, former and present teachers, and others.

According to epidemiologist Dr. Wendy Cozen, cancer may possess numerous causes, and in some forms direct links cannot be completely authenticated. She also noted that certain cancers are easily linked to environmental factors such as smoking and cigarettes, while other cancers less easily lend themselves to discernible causal links.

In an epidemiological study, persons who are sick must be interviewed and asked the same questions. Environmental as well as genetic components should be included and considered: a family history of cancers or related illnesses, the type of cancer, a history of smoking or alcohol abuse, exposure to carcinogens as children, and the period during which they contracted the illness. These are just a few of the necessary considerations. Although forms sent to potential clients by the Masry firm included an in-depth health questionnaire, not every former student was a plaintiff, so that could not be a conclusive study, nor did those plaintiffs represent the entire picture. What about students who spent one year at Beverly or two or three and then left? Were they affected as well? How many children in the family were affected if at all? How would information or data for students who have passed on already be collected? The variables comprise an extensive list and it is a long and tedious process that takes a great deal of time, perseverance, and money to accomplish.

I was told it could cost upwards of half a million dollars to conduct such a study. What was the motivation? If Erin spent the money for a study and it showed no excess existed, it would severely damage her case. If the city ordered it done and excess was proven, that would help Erin prove her charges. It would also take years during which the city would be forced to live in fear over high-school safety. It did not seem either side had a valid motivation for the expense.

However, many others were in favor of conducting one since without such a study, no definitive conclusions about safety or health could truly be discerned. Aside from Kleinman, Ari Bussel proposed that the Beverly Hills High School Alumni Association undertake the task of notifying all former students to gather information in a special database. Despite his insistence, no one was willing to support such an aggressive and exhaustive effort. He then urged the PTA to take on the job, but they were unwilling as well. Bussel believed that without the data, those affected would be unable to uncover information they sought concerning their illnesses.

As the plaintiff numbers mounted so too did questions in the community over the types of cancers and their frequency. Many were afraid. Although they showed no signs of any illness thus far, the future was a concern. Masry asked for ongoing medical monitoring in addition to a financial settlement. He also continued to insist he had evidence to back his claims and was very confident of his legal position, stating, "I'm putting my money where my mouth is. Either come on board and help these children, or else write one big check."

While the attorneys spoke about cancers, other illnesses contributed to plaintiff numbers. At one point during the lawsuits an accounting of the claim forms revealed that of the 216 filed, 98 were cancers and that included four skin cancer claims and a number of autoimmune diseases. Although most plaintiffs had attended the school and were suffering from disease, others' illnesses were not so cut-and-dry, nor were they all a specific sickness, but rather the fear of becoming ill. Most residents I spoke with agreed with Masry that greater oversight of the well was both necessary and the city's responsibility. A six-hundred-page document filed in Superior

Court on January 2, 2004, by the Masry & Vititoe firm included requests for compensation and medical monitoring for illness and future cancer occurrences.

I spoke with some of the plaintiffs ill with diseases other than cancer. One litigant alleged her arthritis was a direct result of the oil emissions from the high school. She sought $5 million for fear of a future diagnosis of cancer as well as medical monitoring. The woman, now residing outside California, learned about the lawsuit through a friend's roommate, who was married to one of the plaintiffs' attorneys. The attorney informed her that autoimmune diseases like arthritis were also at issue and considered part of the lawsuit. The fifty-year-old plaintiff explained to me that her arthritis was premature for her age and was a direct result of the oil well. She believed that her problems maintaining her active lifestyle, which included tennis on a regular basis, were abnormal for her age: "My doctor said if I cut back and play tennis two days a week, I will have less aches and pains, but I choose to live a healthy lifestyle, so I go to physical therapy. I can't understand why I am suffering from these aches and pains. I'm a very healthy person, eat correctly, work out religiously, don't drink excessively, never smoked, have very low blood pressure, and my body is very athletic. It didn't make sense that I should have arthritis and so many pains." Although her doctor recommended Tylenol and cutting back on her activity level, she was adamant that she was the one who was responsible for her lifestyle and chose to remain active without the help of medication.

Another plaintiff, residing in Florida, suffers from Hodgkin's disease. She never attended Beverly Hills schools but intermittently visited her grandparents in the area from 1971 to 1989. She was alleging injury as a result of prolonged exposure to toxic chemicals during these vacation periods.

Now residing outside of California, one plaintiff explained he contracted Hodgkin's after swimming regularly at the high school gym as part of the YMCA program. He stated, "I am curious myself about whether these allegations are true. I don't think they know what causes it." He, as well as many others, expressed a desire to resolve unanswered questions concerning their illnesses and were hopeful the lawsuit would successfully achieve that end.

Others with more dangerous and unusual illnesses also saw the lawsuit as a way to explain their plight. One Beverly Hills graduate and cancer survivor diagnosed with malignant fibrous histiocytoma at the age of twenty-eight spoke candidly about what influenced his decision to join the suit. According to him, his high-grade cancer is very rare for those under sixty years old. "I don't know the answers, but my biggest thing is I'd like to know the truth," he said. "And if there's nothing here, I'll be the first to stand up and say I'm sorry. But first let's find the truth."

His initial reaction to the lawsuit was one of disbelief. "I thought maybe it was just a frivolous lawsuit and someone attempting to get money. The stigma of the Erin Brockovich name was also a problem for me. I thought, 'Oh, another movie.' But for several months people kept calling me and then something just clicked."

He cited two reasons for joining the lawsuit: "The first was the effect on my life. This has been a major change and I haven't stopped worrying since it happened [about] the chance and fear of a recurrence. It is even worse since my daughter was born. Every day I get up and I worry about it. I need to know, and if there is nothing, let them prove that also."

When his daughter was born he was rejected for insurance

and said that pushed him over the edge. "The other thing is the money. I can't get health or life insurance since this happened. Every father worries about their daughter if something should happen to them. I'm willing to donate money to research; I do now, I don't want people suffering and I want to help find a cure. I have a parent who died of cancer."

He claimed no one talked to him about money, only about finding the truth. "I have no way of knowing if I'll get a dime; the lawyers may get everything. But for me, even if I never get a dime, the major concern is to know if this [the oil well] affected my life because no one should suffer through this." It should be noted that this BHHS graduate ultimately received no monies.

After speaking with numerous alumni, including some who declined to join the litigation, I concluded that most were relatively certain the attorneys would, were any money awarded, receive the lion's share. However, the overwhelming concern voiced was that quiet desperation to learn the truth. Like most who suffer from disease, they felt a need to discover some cause or explanation for their plight—especially since so many had been afflicted at a young age.

A plaintiff I have known personally for years is especially troubled by a persistent nausea. The array of doctors with whom she has consulted can find no valid reason for her illness, but she is certain toxic emissions are at the root of her problem. The nausea has impacted her life and she admits frustration over not only the constant suffering but also her need to understand its cause in the hope it will lead to a cure. Other graduates I spoke to also suffer from this mysterious complaint. Thus far no one has sufficiently explained these symptoms or their cause.

Regardless of how many plaintiffs or alumni I interviewed, it was obvious their goal was universal: to find answers regarding their illnesses. I eventually learned that finding truth would be the most difficult task anyone would undertake.

To understand the cancers and their frequency I turned to experts like Dr. Thomas Mack, epidemiologist at the Keck School of Medicine of the University of Southern California Norris, for clarification. He explained the numbers could not be examined unless all data was inputted properly. He stated, "Mr. Masry's claims cannot be examined unless the information is collected, which would give a true and accurate reading."

Dr. Mack said comparisons would not be accurate unless the counting of cases and of persons at risk was done using the same definitions. He explained that cancer registries usually count cases on an annual basis, and the persons at risk are based on the census estimates for that year. However, that approach would not be the most sensible method for this comparison since the concern is about the cases that appeared over a long period of time. "In that circumstance, in order to come up with an estimate of how many cases would ordinarily have occurred, one would need to know exactly how many people were entered into the search each year, and how long each has been followed. The registry rates for each of those years, for the appropriate ages, would then be applied to the number of persons there each year, which means that a single person must be counted at risk for multiple years.

"There are other definition problems, and not only what constitutes a cancer. For example, are cases only counted if the person spent all years in the school, or are they counted if they were only there for a month? If so, then it would be important to know how many people passed through the school, rather than how many graduated. If not, then any case in a person who didn't graduate should be excluded. That's how it should be calculated to get the real denominator."

Among cancers listed at that point were twenty-four thyroid cancers, sixteen Hodgkin's lymphomas, seven non-Hodgkin's lymphomas, nine breast cancers, three leukemia occurrences, eleven testicular cancers, and various others. In some cases patients displayed more than one type of cancer. Dr. Mack's wife, Dr. Cozen, said the numbers were not a surprise. Her expertise as a cancer epidemiologist for USC's Keck Cancer Surveillance Program, specializing in cancer case data collection for the State of California, was helpful. She explained that some types of cancer occur more often in certain neighborhoods. The difficulty lies in deciding whether the increase is occurring by chance or because of a particular exposure.

She explained even if there appears to be an excess, the current accepted theory suggests it may be due to clusters of people with similar lifestyles and other risk factors. "For example, I know that young people of higher socioeconomic status are at a higher risk of developing the most common kind of Hodgkin's disease. The evidence suggests that this is because the risk of young adult Hodgkin's disease is linked to delayed exposure to a common childhood virus, similar to the situation we once saw with paralytic polio, and that we see with infectious mononucleosis today. Children in a more protected environment tend to have fewer siblings and fewer chances of infection and grow up susceptible. When they get the infection as older children, adolescents, or young adults, these infections often have more serious consequences."

I asked Dr. Cozen if it was possible the toxic cocktail of emissions emitting from the oil well and Sempra facility could affect a child's immune system, lowering it and making it more vulnerable to the onset of seemingly related diseases. She said there was no answer to that question because she was unaware any tests of that nature had been conducted. To my own surprise, I have found no studies that test the reaction of a combination of chemicals on children's immune systems.

Dr. Cozen also pointed out that women with higher education levels are at greater risk of breast cancer, supposedly because they tend to have fewer children and have them at a later age. "Early pregnancy, many pregnancies, and long periods of breastfeeding protect against breast cancer. We would not be surprised to find a cluster of either of these types of cancers in Beverly Hills because of what we know about their causes."

She felt it was important for Beverly Hills residents to understand that approximately 34,000 new cases of cancer are diagnosed every year in the residents of Los Angeles County. "Thus cancers do occur, and they occur in all Los Angeles neighborhoods and in the graduates of every high school. We at the USC Keck School of Medicine/Norris Cancer Center have spent the last thirty years studying the causes of cancer in the Los Angeles population. We are aware of no evidence that the cancer incidence in Beverly Hills is higher than in other similar Los Angeles neighborhoods."

She also admitted new studies and information are constantly being added and new conclusions may be reached based on the results of any new study. "We've begun a study of the higher incidence of the thyroid cancers, but I want to point out that the rise is not specific to Beverly Hills, but all of West Los Angeles and the United States. We are looking into the cause of this increase. I also think it is important to note that cancers such as skin and melanomas are caused by exposure to the sun, not oil emissions."

I asked Ed Masry about the additional non-cancerous cases, and he said it was typical in these types of lawsuits to receive other types of complaints as well. Among allegations naming the oil well as a cause were ulcerated tonsils, insomnia, dizziness, memory loss, tingling sensations, nosebleeds, heart problems, Bell's palsy, hearing and vision difficulties, balance problems, difficulties in concentration, urinary problems, gastrointestinal irregularities, and numerous sinus complaints. The more plaintiffs who signed on, the more it became apparent how difficult and exhaustive an epidemiological study would be and why neither side was willing to take on the task.

"It is such a shame no one ever undertook the study for now we will never know the truth," Kleinman told me. She was not the only one who expressed a desire to find the truth, and to this day plaintiffs remain disappointed that efforts to learn the causes of their illness were never successful.

Eric Umansky, author of an investigative article about the lawsuit for *New Republic* magazine, was not surprised by the city's claims or the plaintiff lawyers' admissions. "In my piece, I noted multiple cases where Brockovich and Masry allege there is an excess of health problems or toxins and when asked to present the data are unable to do so."

I personally was privy to such an occurrence. A few years after Erin's initial foray into the city, I received a call from the superintendent of a school district outside of Palm Springs, California. She was quite distraught over a report on the local Palm Springs CBS station the night before alleging Erin had secretly taken samples from the grounds on one of their schools and discovered excessive cancer-causing toxins. The scenario rang a familiar bell. Apparently, several teachers in the school had become afflicted with cancer, believed the number was excessive, and consulted Erin. The superintendent was shocked and disturbed by what she referred to as "these tactics," and knowing Beverly Hills and its schools were currently embroiled in a legal battle, she was seeking advice.

I referred her to then BHHS superintendent Jeff Hubbard. Interestingly, things turned out quite differently for that district. Hubbard advised that school board to conduct testing immediately and they ultimately found no correlation with Erin's alleged levels. Brockovich disappeared and was not heard from again, at least not there.

I phoned the CBS affiliate at the time and asked the reporter if she had investigated the allegations before breaking the story. She admitted she possessed no information and had not checked out Erin's allegations. She said she would look into the situation and call me with more information, but I never received any updates.

This was not the only time I was personally contacted about Erin's visits to other cities. The calls always featured the same scenario but I was focused on Beverly Hills issues. As far as I know none of those who contacted me became high-profile cases that surfaced in the media. One disturbing aspect of the case was the looming question of whether or not the levels at the school, although within normal ranges most of the time, were truly safe. The increasing number of claims seemed to cast suspicion on the accepted levels, and the fact that such standards are consistently being revised did little to ensure everyone the well was not a health threat and had never been a danger. The prospect of new information coming to light in the future was unsettling to many.

Most voiced concerns about the wisdom of placing an oil well on school property, and Ari Bussel was angry about what he believed was improper regulation. "The oil wells are no longer as full or rich and now everyone is looking, carefully, with a microscope as litigation looms overhead. Let us be realistic—can anything go wrong? And even if it did, what would happen, another slap on the hand?"

Officials complained that constant discussions between city officials and the school board in both open and closed sessions were an ongoing distraction. The frustration level surrounding the city's attempts to conduct business grew higher and eventually Superintendent Dr. Gwen Gross and City Manager Mark Scott left for other cities. This was a price paid by the community for the ongoing disruption and fear.

Dr. Gross confessed her career as an administrator could be better served on more worthwhile efforts, not lawsuits and attorney posturing. "I only had so many years left to fulfill my dreams as an educator. I didn't want to fill them with lawyers and court battles." She moved on and is now superintendent of schools in Irvine, California.

Scott also admitted he felt stifled and believed the problems inherent in fighting the lawsuit robbed valuable time and resources from the city's ability to confront daily issues. He insisted the city and school district went beyond what was necessary in regards to testing. "We were so careful, we even ordered extra tests when traces of arsenic were found along the fence line left by the lawn care company. We knew it was normal to find arsenic in weed killer, but we just wanted to be certain it had nothing whatsoever to do with the oil well."

Scott said listening to Erin telling media the city was negligent concerning their children was frustrating and difficult. "I just couldn't believe the things Erin was saying, when they just weren't true in any way. She was on television talking about me and I'm thinking, 'This isn't me. I know me, and I know I wouldn't do those things.'"

Scott said the lawsuit contributed to his leaving Beverly Hills for a new position. "We were spending so much time and effort on this frivolous, ridiculous lawsuit, it just wasn't fun anymore. It used to bother me a great deal listening to the parents yelling at city attorney Larry Wiener. I think they owe him an apology now."

Scott initially took a job on the East Coast but recently accepted the city manager position in Culver City, California. He has since returned to his hometown of Fresno to be closer to family.

7

Clearing the Air

A subtle thought that is in error may yet give rise to fruitful inquiry that can establish truths of great value.

—Isaac Asimov

While most parents remained in the background, allowing a few generals to emerge, a couple with a more specific agenda, Dr. Abraham W. and his wife Marrina, joined the fray on the front lines. Convinced the potential danger from the wells was radiation, they were certain personal experience would support their theory. Marrina and Dr. W., a professor of internal medicine at the University of California, Los Angeles and staff physician at Cedars-Sinai, have two daughters; one had graduated from BHHS and the other had not yet attended the high school.

The couple believed the variety of medical ailments from which their daughters suffered was directly related to radiation emissions. Plagued by colds and their younger daughter's history of convulsions, they tested the girls for toxins and were shocked to find uranium levels in their systems to be almost three times the usual amount. Setting out to prove that radiation was the culprit, they argued for an investigation into radioactive materials routinely injected into oil wells as part of the extraction process, like iodine 131. Add to this the potential for radon gas spilling as a result of the oil drilling, and it could prove a deadly combination.

On more than one occasion they reiterated their theory that uranium can cause lung cancer and, when swallowed, kidney damage. They were positive the cancers in alumni and local residents were linked to radiation levels at the wells. As tempting as it was to accept their theory, it seemed to fall apart when one took into account the fact that the couple's younger daughter had not yet attended the high school. Undeterred, they attributed the cause to the high levels abundant in the air. This presented two relevant questions: were radiation levels higher than normal and could radon gas even be linked to such illnesses?

The expert I called upon to help me understand radiation levels and their potential part in the oil well equation was Kathleen Kaufman, director of Radiation Management at the L.A. County Department of Health Services. Kaufman was generous with her time and expertise and examined the situation at the high school closely. When contacted, Kaufman said that she saw nothing relating to the use of radioactive iodine 131 on this site that would cause her concern. "I can only address use of radioactive iodine 131 based on what I know occurred there," she said. "I don't see any risk to anyone in the adjacent community." Kaufman based her opinion on what she had learned from Venoco and the licensee who injects the iodine. She said there are certain tests and standards to which the company who injects the iodine must adhere and they are tested yearly.

The result of radiation testing by L.A. County to allay residents' fears was announced at a school board meeting by new Superintendent of Schools Jeffrey Hubbard. Citing results from Kaufman, Hubbard explained there was no elevation in the normal radiation background levels at the school, either indoors or outside on the field. The department's Radiological Management branch had visited the high school and the adjacent Venoco oil well site and, using various methods and equipment, technicians collected data from the oil well site, the high-school softball field, the outdoor basketball courts, the athletic field, and numerous locations within school buildings. For comparison, data was also collected at an empty lot approximately one mile southwest (and upwind) of the campus. Kaufman concluded the numbers were within normal ranges and nothing indicated radiation concentrations above standard Los Angeles background levels.

According to Venoco vice president Mike Edwards, only three wells were injected and the injector holds two millicures of radiation. Kaufman explained, "We did an analysis and if ten millicures spilled—and to our knowledge this has never occurred—the radiation exposure in their injector would be the suspension of iodine into the atmosphere in one square meter about one millirem at the fence line between the oil pumping site and the BHHS campus. This is one one-hundredth of the annual public dose limit allowed, which is 100 millirems a year." She added that those figures did not take into account the twenty-foot fence dividing the properties, which would further reduce the dose and hamper air movement. "If a student or adult were standing where the spill occurred at the borderline between the high school and oil well site, the exposure would only be one millirem."

Background radiation exposure to those living in the L.A. area is 300 millirems a year as a result of cosmic radiation from the sun, moon, stars, and naturally occurring radioactive materials in the soil. Kaufman also pointed out that the dose of radiation from an airplane trip to New York could be up to five millirems. "If you travel to other parts of the world or the country, like Denver, the radiation exposure is even greater because of increased levels at higher elevations. We don't have a lot of uranium in the soil here in California compared to other parts of the world." Not only found in naturally occurring radiation, iodine 131 is commonly used for nuclear medical procedures and as a treatment for thyroid cancers and hyperthyroidism. "When treating a thyroid cancer, 100 to 200 millicures of iodine will often be given in treatment."

Hubbard told the school board, "Regarding radon, the department's testing found the concentrations inside school buildings to be lower than the U.S. Environmental Protection Agency's action level for indoor radon. I hope the information is helpful to the school community and puts concerns about radiation to rest. The latest survey of the high school and oil well operation is the second by a government agency to conclude that the oil and gas poses no unusual health risks at Beverly Hills High School.

"Like the South Coast Air Quality Management District's report and the reports of the independent environmental testing firm Camp, Dresser, and McKee, the report by the state Department of Health Services is available for public review at the school district's offices."

These public announcements became a regular part of school board and city council meetings, but they did not reassure fearful parents or deter the trial attorneys from their appointed rounds. When asked in court about the seemingly safe report Beverly Hills received, Al Stewart of Baron and Budd law firm commented, "Based on my clients' experiences and the ongoing regulatory problems,

I've seen nothing that would convince me to send my kids to that school."

Concern about radiation was highlighted when it was announced that new iodine 131 testing would be necessary at the well site. According to Venoco vice president Mike Edwards, the problem arose when "after completing the radioactive tracer surveys on the water injection wells, one of the wells began to show pressure in the casing. We shut the well and scheduled a work over rig. The rig attempted to pull the tubing and packer from the well, but the packer remained solidly in the casing. The tubing joint above the packer eventually broke, leaving the packer in place 7,150 feet down the well."

Edwards added that work on the one water injection well had caused a stoppage, but the rest of the facility was operational. He explained that a new packer was sleeved over the existing packer, allowing water to be injected as it had been before. "The regulations require the new packer to be inspected with a radioactive tracer survey. The tracer survey is not currently scheduled, but we hope to in the next several weeks."

He described the injection process and said the tracer injection could take two to three days, depending on how the operation proceeded and barring any mechanical problems. "The tool is delivered in a pickup truck, already assembled. It's lowered into the well and connected to cables and the whole tool is lowered to a depth over a mile deep. Then, minute amounts of iodine are released from the tool while being measured by a detector."

Additional data also monitored by the tool includes temperature gauges relayed back to the surface, Edwards continued. The operator of the tool wears a badge showing how much, if any, radiation he may be exposed to during the process. Iodine is shielded in a container and the tool is loaded at another location. He stressed that the company handling the injection process is fully licensed and reports to a central state agency in Sacramento.

The iodine 131 injected into the wells every two years serves as a tracer to ensure there is no leakage and is mandated by the State of California. Floyd Leeson, then of the Division of Oil, Gas, and Geothermal Resources (DOGGR) verified the necessity for the iodine's use to determine well leaks, ensuring the water-injection wells functioned properly. According to Edwards, at that time there were sixteen oil-producing wells and two water-injection wells, with a possible third coming on board.

Parents had asked to be informed and it was announced the radioactive iodine 131 would be injected during spring break when the students were on vacation. Kathleen Kaufman would also be present during the injection to take new radioactive measurements while the wells were functioning.

The day of the test, April 5, 2004, arrived and at 8 A.M. Jody Kleinman and I arrived to witness the process firsthand, she to cast a watchful, mistrusting eye and I, I guess, out of curiosity and a desire to report it accurately. Perhaps it stemmed from the same instinct that kicks in when you pass a car accident and can't help but sneak a peek. I'm inclined to believe it is the latter. There were also representatives from DOGGR, Venoco, Welaco (a company that services oil fields), the L.A. County and state departments of health, the school district's environmentalist Mark Katchen of the Phylmar group, the school board's attorney Bill Ireland, and Dr. Abraham and Marrina W. No Beverly Hills city officials or school board members were present, and although it was not required they be on site, I was beginning to feel a tad resentful that no radioactivity would be pointed in their direction.

Two white pickup trucks with a long arm fed the tube down six thousand feet into the ground to begin the pumping process. As we looked on, some mumbled in anger and frustration. The men in white hazmat suits grinned with amusement at the worried looks on our faces. Jody and I felt they should have at least had the decency to feign concern.

Dr. W. and Marrina listened intently as Edwards explained the process, but their demeanor displayed their suspicions about the safety or wisdom of having radioactive materials so close to the children's play area. "When patients of mine who are BHHS students and alumni are asking me for medical advice, I cannot reassure them that they were not affected by the oil wells," Dr. W. told me. "Especially now, after we have seen with our own eyes the harsh reality at the site." I stared at the oil wells and wondered why attempts to protect our children are not as strong as those to protect wildlife in Alaska, marine life from offshore oil drilling, or even chickens.

We exchanged worried looks, surprised to see the reading on the radiation monitors rising. Kaufman informed us she read in her radiation monitor 140 microrems, fourteen times more than the background radiation (5-10 microrems per hour). The only readings were supposed to be background levels because the containers were alleged to be completely sealed. The walls surrounding the site interrupted any air flow, and Jody and I silently prayed for a gust of wind to push the radioactivity away from us. Marrina described the scene as "unreal." I pretended I wasn't alarmed at watching a truck loaded with radioactive materials park under an oil well rig just a few feet away from the high school's bleachers. We stood silently at an industrial site with eighteen oil wells under our feet spewing fumes and odors that made us lightheaded and holding radiation monitors with rising readings. Inside, I fought the urge to jump the fence and run screaming across the field. Reassurances of the well's safety were lost to me beneath some imagined cloud of powerful radiation. It may have existed only in my imagination, but the lines were quickly beginning to blur. We were not allowed to videotape or photograph, but there is no doubt all parents should witness the process with their own eyes.

A monitor on a truck at the site contained equipment that read the injection tube as it moved through the ground, catching any spikes in radiation levels. Kaufman monitored the process, checking for radioactive levels in the air, both at the site and inside the high school. She explained that if you moved away from the immediate area the radiation levels dropped significantly, returning to background readings. "I've not seen anything at that site that would indicate that there is a radiological concern," she told me. "We're still waiting for some results from the two canisters for air samples we set up near the work area and the additional radon canisters placed inside the school, as well as by the track and basketball fields. Those will take a few weeks to read and the outside canisters will be picked up today."

Kaufman said if parents would adhere to the science they would be more comfortable with the safety of the site's radiation levels. Although she continued efforts to reassure us, we all felt a bit queasy and skeptical, convinced one wave of our hands could now light up lamps and start blenders as we passed. The look on Jody Kleinman's face mirrored my own as our monitor numbers continued to rise.

According to Kaufman, at approximately twenty-five feet from the injector truck, background radiation levels dropped to normal—less than one millirem per hour. The law requires exposure rates in an uncontrolled area be no more than two millirems an hour. "No one said there wouldn't be any exposure in the area," Kaufman said. "We were expecting low exposure rates and that's what we found. If you are going to have more than two millirems in an hour, the law requires barriers to be erected so that no member of the public can be within that two-millirem area. There is a brick wall made of concrete separating the field from the site. Concrete is a material that is used to shield x-ray therapy rooms. One dental x-ray on the skin surface is about 300 millirems and a full mouth dental set is eighteen exposures. Part of the reason they are higher is because they are x-raying through bone."

Kaufman said the issue of whether or not the dose levels are high or not is a controversial problem because it isn't possible to conduct studies on humans. You cannot expose people to radiation and wait and see if they get cancer. Studies done now are on massive doses of radioactivity, and other studies at lower levels are done on animals. Visions of lab rats running around glowing like light bulbs danced through my head.

Canisters were placed in the high school to check the results from the radon testing the previous fall. "We are repeating tests because sometimes levels can vary from season to season," Kaufman explained. "There was no problem with the last test results and they were well within safe EPA guidelines. We saw nothing that causes us concern."

Floyd Leeson, oil and gas engineer for the Department of Oil, Gas, and Geothermal Resources, assured me, "Residents should know that we are overseeing Venoco's operations on a weekly and monthly basis and believe they are doing what is needed to stay in compliance. This company has even won awards." He said a printout with specific levels and readings is made to inform engineers of any residual radioactivity at the site before the process begins. The entire injection, which took approximately three hours to complete, is repeated every two years. However, Edwards said, the process can take up to three days when there are glitches in the application.

When I asked whether or not the iodine can affect the groundwater, Leeson explained that there is a barrier of natural rock at approximately two hundred feet below the surface that precludes the iodine from leeching into the groundwater.

Radiation testing continued and results reflected normal levels at the wells. One official report analyzing the previous season's testing stated that "in August and September of this year, DHS/RHB [the Radiologic Health Branch within the Food, Drug, and Radiation Safety Division of the Department of Public Health] performed radiological surveys at the BHHS site, including the Venoco oil well site and the BHHS campus, and the results of these measurements were reviewed by LAC/DHS [Los Angeles County Department of Health Services]. The surveys included a radiation mapping survey to determine if there were elevated radiation levels in the top six through 12 inches of soil, laboratory analysis of soil samples to determine radioactive concentrations in the soil, and an evaluation of radon levels indoors at the BHHS campus, and outdoors at the Venoco site and the BHHS campus."

The results of each of these measurements were compared to a nearby control site or to normal background radiation levels. "Background radiation is present virtually everywhere, throughout the environment, so no concern is warranted where radiation levels do not exceed those found in the local, unaffected environment.

"In summary, no radiation levels or radioactive materials were identified above normal background levels at BHHS. Based on a review of the oil well site operational history, the survey results, and the laboratory results, there is no evidence that the Venoco site has caused an increase in radioactive materials or radiation either on the BHHS campus, or at the Venoco site adjacent to the campus."

Despite the apparent "all clear" agencies continued to sound concerning the site, Dr. W. and other residents requested that inexpensive radiation monitors be placed at the school, to no avail. "A single testing procedure is not significant," W. concluded. "A monitoring procedure was not established. In addition, the pipes, where radioactive materials might accumulate, were replaced again, for the second time within a year, right before the testing. This is an insult to the intelligence of the people of Beverly Hills."

Councilmembers assured parents that all tests taken thus far had shown the wells to be safe. "We have tested extensively and have discussed the radioactive iodine 131," one member said. "We will continue testing until we are certain there is no danger to the students or residents of this community."

Even as the radiation test results were being returned, attorneys met in Los Angeles Superior Court and a hearing was scheduled to address the AQMD subpoena from the Masry and Baron and Budd law firms. Meanwhile, Judge Wendell Mortimer ruled that the plaintiffs had met the required criteria, enabling the case against Beverly Hills and the oil companies to proceed.

In the midst of the turmoil, Venoco's vice president, Mike Edwards, remained positive. "We share the community's concern to have reliable, scientific information to evaluate claims of health concerns. We are glad to see that this extensive radiation testing shows our site and the school campus are safe." The impact of those positive results were reinforced when Venoco submitted its health risk assessment (HRA) to the AQMD, showing a less than one in a million risk of cancer at the site.

The community had been eagerly awaiting the HRA and was anxious to hear the agency's evaluation. AQMD executive director Dr. Barry Wallerstein attempted to explain the process for reviewing the health risk assessment and the criteria used: "This is a full-blown health risk assessment for air pollutant emissions from the entire facility. The testing company takes air emissions from all their equipment and then utilizes computer models to estimate the risk to the surrounding community." Wallerstein said the AQMD would focus on checking the data input into the model and scrutinize the model itself to ensure that the results generated were correct. The AQMD would then insert the same data into its own modeling program to ensure the results could be duplicated. "The AQMD has put a high priority on the analysis of the assessment and hope to have the preliminary results in a few weeks."

For the HRA, samples of well gases were also taken inside the well before they were released into the air. Wallerstein noted that sampling the well gases would determine the concentration at the pumps, compressors, valves, and the amine unit, thus addressing the community's concern over levels of volatile organic compounds potentially released by vapor leaks and gas leaks.

The assessment was prepared in accordance with both the October 1993 California Air Pollution Control Officers Association Air Toxics "Hot Spots" Program Risk Assessment Guidelines and the July 1996 AQMD Supplemental Guidelines for Preparing Risk Assessments. These must comply with the Air Toxics "Hot Spots" Information and Assessment Act

(AB2588), Version 2.1. The document includes an emissions inventory of detected AB2588 listed compounds and a comprehensive analysis of the dispersion of emissions, the potential for human exposure, and a quantitative assessment of both individual and population-wide health risks associated with the predicted levels of exposure. Table one reports that the facility emissions were estimated to result in an increased cancer risk of less than 1 per million to the maximally exposed individual resident and less than 0.01 per million to the maximally exposed individual worker. According to the report, the calculated maximum individual cancer risk did not exceed the significant risk level of 100 per million or the action risk level of 25 per million, as established by the South Coast Air Quality Management District. In addition, the calculated maximum incremental cancer risk does not exceed the total facility risk level of 10 per million. According to Atwood, at 25 in a million, Venoco would be told to mitigate and at 30 in a million, they would have to notify the public.

AQMD senior engineer Marcia Baverman, who worked on the health risk assessment, said Environmental Audit, Inc., the company who performed the HRA, has a wide client base including defense contractors, oil companies, developers, vehicle manufacturers, and hotel and casino operators. The company was founded in 1979 to provide hazardous substances and waste management services, environmental planning, and land use, including compliance with the California Environmental Quality Act, health risk assessments, air quality management and permitting, water quality management, and regulatory compliance.

Mike Edwards commented on the assessment, saying, "Venoco, in response to a directive from the South Coast Air Quality Management District, today submitted a comprehensive health risk assessment for its oil and gas operation adjacent to Beverly Hills High School. The health risk assessment was performed by an independent expert and was based on scientific testing conducted at the oil and gas facility. The risk assessment provides worst-case estimates of potential public health risk.

"Even given the worst case exposure assumptions set forth in the report, the risk assessment concluded that there is no significant risk to students at the high school, residents of Beverly Hills, or people who work near the facility.

"Worst case exposure assumptions include the assumption that students are standing on the football field/track exposed to the Venoco facility twenty-four hours a day for 70 years. The health risk assessment results are well below the facility risk levels established by regulation, reconfirming the previous scientific air quality testing completed at the site to date. The AQMD will now review the risk assessment and its findings."

Simply put, at the end of all the testing, examining, and assessments, it was shown the site was ultimately within accepted risk limits.

8

Glamorous Beverly Hills

*We are made wise not by the recollection of our past, but by
the responsibility for our future.*

—George Bernard Shaw

All the comings, goings, and attention beg the question,
What is there about Beverly Hills that attracts and repels so
many? How did oil and glamour mix to create an aroma that
captivated and enticed the rich and famous, and sometimes
infamous, to its borders? Attempting to explain its obvious
cache, one notices that there are three Beverly Hills faces, all
distinct and interesting in their own way. Together they make
up what is one of the most famous and recognizable cities on
the planet. No understanding of the dynamics of its appeal
could be complete without a quick explanation of the city's
split personality.

A name guaranteed to impress in most civilized corners of
the world, Beverly Hills wears its first and most obvious image
of wealth and celebrity like the couture gowns that grace the
windows of its famous Rodeo Drive shops. Beverly Hills High
School itself has served up over the years a hefty portion of
superstar attendees and graduates that reads like a who's who

of Hollywood and Washington. Just a partial list includes Jack Abramoff, Corbin Bernsen, Albert Brooks, Nicolas Cage, Richard Chamberlain, Jackie Cooper, Jamie Lee Curtis, Richard Dreyfuss, Nora Ephron, Carrie Fisher, California Supreme Court justice Ronald M. George, Gina Gershon, Melissa Gilbert, Joel Grey, H. R. Haldeman, Angelina Jolie, David Kohan, Monica Lewinsky, Lyle and Erik Menendez, Breckin Meyer, Laraine Newman, André Previn, Rain Pryor, Rob Reiner, Antonio Sabato Jr., David Schwimmer, Pauly Shore, Simpsons creator Sam Simon, Jonathan Silverman, Alicia Silverstone, Slash, Tori Spelling, and Betty White.

Yet, a simple list of graduates can't begin to explain the mystique that draws an Erin Brockovich to Beverly Hills. In an interview on NBC's *Today Show* with Matt Lauer and Shelly Smith on March 22, 2001, before the Beverly Hills lawsuit, Smith made an interesting comment while speaking with Erin. Following Erin's question, "Do you think for one minute we ever thought there was going to be a $333 million settlement? And have I ever stopped to think, 'Oh, gee, they're going to make a movie about it, star Julia Roberts, name it after me, and then give me $2 million bonus to boot'?" Smith replied, "That settlement changed her life. She bought a million-dollar home, drives a gold Jag, and gets her three-thousand-dollar silk suits custom made in Beverly Hills."

Even with its connection to money, it is something far more enticing than temporal fame and fortune that leads seekers to the city's borders. The allure has a supernatural or spiritual link to fame that haunts and enhances the city's famous mystique. A walk down any Beverly Hills street conjures the aura of Hollywood past, hovering as an invisible cloak over the homes of previous inhabitants. The name Roxbury Drive elicits images of Lucille Ball, Jimmy Stewart, and more recently Angelina Jolie, who shared a home on the 800 block with Billy Bob Thornton. One can almost hear the sound of piano music wafting through the windows of the Roxbury home of George Gershwin as he wrote and performed his timeless masterpieces or the voice of Jack Benny relaxing in his upstairs sitting room, laughing hysterically at George Burns' latest practical joke.

The parade of tour busses slowly cruising the city's streets pass historic palaces like Grayhall Mansion, where Douglas Fairbanks and Mary Pickford rendezvoused in a secret tunnel during their love affair. Marion Davies shared a home on Lexington Drive with William Randolph Hearst, and Milton Berle hosted the first star-studded Oscar party at his house on North Crescent Drive.

Passing the Linden Drive home of Bugsy Siegel's girlfriend Virginia Hill, one can imagine the sounds of bullets blasting through the living room window shortly before midnight in the infamous murder that ended the life of Beverly Hills' most notorious, yet visionary gangster. Or perhaps visitors can relive the moment the body of Johnny Stompanato was carried out of Lana Turner's Bedford Drive home after her daughter Cheryl stabbed and killed the man threatening her glamorous mother.

Memories of Phil Silvers walking to La Scala for chopped salad or to Nate 'n Al for corned beef—favorite foods for the regular weekend-long poker games he hosted that included such notables as Robert Redford and Paul Newman—coincide with ethereal visions of superstar Gene Kelly playing in Will Rogers Park with his kids. If one listens carefully while walking along North Beverly Drive, two of its most famous residents can be heard practicing their songs together from *The Wizard of Oz*. The ghosts of Jack Haley and Ray Bolger may still be following the yellow brick road even now.

These former occupants of Beverly Hills left more than a history; they left a legacy that draws people to their doorsteps. Beverly Hills has, in a word, "created" an image that remains a public relations coup. Those who arrive in Beverly Hills do so with a desire to touch and absorb a bit of that aura and to take home a scintilla of that magical glamour. To store it in their memory banks for that rainy day fantasy when they are washing windows or cleaning the attic. To inhale like a heady spray of fine perfume the scent of a lifestyle they have not lived, an era they never witnessed and to rub elbows with people they would never know. Yet, this glamorous reputation may also serve as a double-edged sword when outsiders wish to exploit its fame.

Researching the oil well case, I was struck by one significant truth: facts take on a different perspective when a celebrity disseminates information. America has adopted a belief system predicated on the assumption that the more rich and famous the speaker, the more credible the statement. We imbue those who have learned to deliver a line or a song with some supernatural intelligence they rarely possess. By raising them beyond their intellectual capacity, we forfeit our own good sense. Thus, it wasn't surprising that when Erin Brockovich spoke loudly and in grandiose terms of the death and disease perpetrated by the City of Beverly Hills, hundreds flocked to her message.

That Brockovich's lawsuit against the city, its schools, and the power and oil companies was so emotionally charged, environmentally relevant, and star studded made it fodder for celebrity watchers. The adversaries were focused, high profile, and richly endowed with both detractors and fanatical fans. Beverly Hills, Erin Brockovich, and Big Oil—a formidable trio tangling and wrangling over Beverly Hills bucks.

The characters in the drama read like a casting director's dream, and one of its stars is a city of approximately thirty-five thousand with a high profile and wealth that far exceeds its small town status. Beverly Hills is actually a 5.7-square-mile city whose daytime population balloons to more than 200,000. Despite myth and legend, there are roughly one thousand non-celebrity movers and shakers in Beverly Hills and five hundred or so who call the shots. Celebrities have little vested interest in the city's politics or welfare since they no longer send their children to the public schools, nor do they join the PTA or shop the neighborhood grocery store.

This leads us to another part of that famous face: everyday life in Beverly Hills. Although most believe otherwise, the streets of the city are not populated with movie stars trolling for the latest fashions at Gucci or Dior. Although occasionally one will have a "movie star sighting," the numerous high-profile residents within the city's borders remain securely ensconced behind gates and seldom appear on the city's public streets. In these times of paparazzi attacks and stalkers it falls to stylists and personal assistants to tend to the mundane errands of the rich and famous, while most chic stores deliver to and generously accommodate their celebrity clientele.

There are exceptions, however. Nate 'n Al is still the deli of choice for those who wish to saunter out in public view for a corned beef fix, and Spago still offers up a healthy serving of celebrities on a daily basis. The Grill, Peninsula Bar, and other "in" spots boast the possibility of a front row seat as a "deal" goes down or an agency lures away a big Hollywood fish. Celebrity sightings might include Madonna riding her bike down a quiet street or Jay Leno pulling up on his motorcycle to run into Pioneer Hardware. Yes, that's even Erin Brockovich entering an exclusive Beverly Hills shop to have her suits custom made after her financial windfall from PG&E.

At times, it is possible to see a star rushing through Neiman Marcus, Saks, or North Face for a purchase or a pair of shoes, but on the whole the designers du jour like Fendi, Gucci, and Chanel depend on some locals and a high influx of international tourists to make their quotas. Many young and chic celebs are more visible at the trendy boutiques on Robertson Boulevard, which exists within Los Angeles' borders.

Although each night the city's party venues host glamorous galas and events at such formidable spots as the Beverly Hilton or the Beverly Hills Hotel, stars who attend do so to promote a favorite charity, lend their name to the organizer's list to elicit funds, receive an honor or award, entertain, or be paid for their appearance. On most mornings, by contrast, Rodeo Drive is actually a quiet street. The stores don't open their expensive eyes until ten and, except for the occasional jogger or early-rising tourist, the city is still wiping the sleep from its plastic-surgery-lifted eyes.

But, on February 6, 2003, Beverly Hills received a surprise wake-up call that brought it abruptly to its Manolo Blahnik-clad feet. That was the day "Green Queen" Erin Brockovich focused her high-profile cleavage on the city's Prada-lined pockets like an implanted, botoxed blonde sets her sights on an aging millionaire. When news of the alleged cancers hit the airwaves, the ripple effects were as large as a tsunami through a city that formerly prided itself on its quiet, elegant demeanor.

Accustomed to a high-profile image, Beverly Hills is no stranger to the effects of its glamorous reputation on those who visit its gold-lined streets each year. After all, it is that reputation that continues to secure its fortunes. Visions of a celebrity lifestyle, filled with parties, luncheons, spas, and vacations, hover like a cloud around its aura. Perfectly coifed and lifted socialites and stars dressed in couture with wide-brimmed hats supposedly nibble calorie-conscious goodies at garden parties behind massively gated, lushly planted mansions. The Beverly Hills Hotel stands in pink glory as a testament to an era of Hollywood opulence and excitement that most have never experienced. But therein lies the rub. For every one of those women who lunch there are women who work. For each socialite there is a career woman and for every spa-goer, a soccer mom. This is its everyday face, the normal, down–to-earth personality visitors never see.

A reputation for wealth and affluence is an enticing target for those whose sights are set on expansive publicity and the multitudes of capital they believe the city affords. Observers are not surprised when outsiders clamor to Beverly Hills' borders to bask in its fame and even collect a bit of its fortune for their private coffers. Business deals must be consummated in a Beverly Hills restaurant to raise their status. Wannabees crowd the outside cafés to be seen and noticed. Egos are massaged by its glossy aura. Self-esteem lifted by humming within its busyness. Its appeal is undisputed and although those who live and exist there each day have grown oblivious to its fame, outsiders do not.

The third face of Beverly Hills is the gritty past all cities share: the original settlers who battled against difficult odds to tame the land. Beverly Hills possesses this rather pragmatic side as well.

Long before the city existed as a bastion of capitalism, Spanish explorers in the mid-1700s named the Beverly Hills area El Rodeo de las Aguas, "gathering of the waters." The water supply was a result of the rain and moisture concentrated in its three canyons—

Franklin, Benedict, and Coldwater—which formed streams and flowed down toward what became Sunset Boulevard and Beverly Drive. Extremely fertile, the area boasted abundant crops of wild oats, cucumber, buckwheat, cress, and prickly pear as well as an array of colorful flora.

Early wars between the area's Native American Tongvas and the European colonizers led to Spanish settlements displacing the native inhabitants, and interestingly, feminism wound up playing a major role in the city's growth. In 1838, California's Mexican governor deeded the land known as El Rancho to Maria Rita Valdez Villa, the gutsy widow of a Spanish soldier. Valdez Villa built a home at the intersection of what today are Sunset Boulevard and Alpine Drive and to further her dream of becoming a cattle and horse rancher, she hired an army of cowboys to work her land.

In those days one's livestock freely grazed across the area, then once a year a rodeo was held at the corner of Pico and Robertson Boulevards to round up the herds. Following one of these roundups, three Native Americans ambushed Maria's ranch. A subsequent shootout at the corner of what became Benedict Canyon and Chevy Chase Drive caused fate to intervene in the widow's plans. Although Maria survived the siege, she was worn down by the constant challenges of cattle ranching. Two years later she sold her land to Benjamin D. Wilson and Henry Hancock for four thousand dollars. The two were also unsuccessful as ranchers and later wiped out by a drought. However, their names live on today as Mt. Wilson and Hancock Park.

The Beverly Hills landscape changed once again following the Civil War when an influx of wildcatters and roughnecks dotted the landscape with oil derricks. Meanwhile, a steady succession of new developers attempted to settle the area but ultimately were all defeated by drought. Enter Burton Green. In 1900, the same year the oil rich wells on which Venoco Oil now sits was discovered, he and his partners purchased the area for the Amalgamated Oil Company. They originally initiated more drilling, but in 1906 after failing to strike oil, they formed the Rodeo Land and Water Company to develop real estate. After reading of Beverly Farms, Massachusetts, in a newspaper, Green proposed they rename the town they were about to build. Thus, Beverly Hills was christened.

Green hired landscape architect Wilbur D. Cook to create a vision and Cook's design included wide, curving, hill-hugging streets, an array of colorful flowers, and sprawling lots to accommodate sprawling, elegant homes. Crescent, Canon, Beverly, Rodeo, Camden, Bedford, Roxbury, and Linden Drives; Carmelita, Elevado, and Lomitas Avenues; and Burton Way, the city's first streets, were officially mapped in 1907. Cook's vision was expanded to include a three-block-long, eighty-foot-wide green area along the north side of Santa Monica Boulevard he named Santa Monica Park; it is now known as Beverly Gardens.

As the new city grew in size and stature, it became apparent that a meeting place to gather and dine was needed and in 1912, one of Beverly Hills' most prestigious landmarks was raised. The Beverly Hills Hotel, or "Pink Palace," quickly became the social center of the city's elegant lifestyle and the place for movie stars and moguls to be seen. Today the hotel's Polo Lounge remains a "happening place" for Hollywood moguls to wheel and deal. Mrs. Margaret Anderson, a high-profile Los Angeles social matron from the Hollywood Hotel, was lured away to manage the new opulent addition. The Pink Palace flourished and soon church services, all formal events, weddings, and even a motion picture theater drew steady streams of Beverly Hills glitterati into its grand ballroom. Ironic indeed that ninety-one years later Erin Brockovich would hold her lawsuit meeting in that same elegant Crystal Ballroom.

Access into the city became easier with the streetcar line running along Sunset Boulevard, and in January 1914, Beverly Hills was incorporated. The city's glamorous reputation began to grow and its first grand Hollywood estate arrived in 1919. Superstars Douglas Fairbanks and Mary Pickford bought land on Summit Drive to build their estate, Pickfair. Immediately a cluster of superstar residences began dotting the landscape. Hollywood legends Harold Lloyd, John Barrymore, Robert Montgomery, Miriam Hopkins, Charlie Chaplin, Tom Mix, Carl Laemmle, Ronald Colman, King Vidor, Buster Keaton, Jack Warner, Clara Bow, Marion Davies, Harry Cohn, and even Rudolph Valentino were among the first rich and famous to build mansions in the new glamour capital of the West.

Will Rogers, the city's first and only honorary mayor, commented on the city's instant land boom in 1923 saying, "Lots are sold so quickly and often out here that they put through escrow made out to the 12th owner. . . . They couldn't possibly make out a separate deed for each purchaser; besides, he wouldn't have time to read it in the 10 minutes' time he owned the land." Rogers is credited with promoting construction of a new city hall in 1932 and a United States post office in 1924. Today the Beverly Hills Cultural Center is housed in the city's second post office, built in 1934.

Now possessing a national reputation, the city also became an "in" place for sports and publicity seekers. The Beverly Hills Speedway, a one and a quarter mile wood oval track on the south side of Wilshire Boulevard between Beverly and Lasky Drives, drew crowds and radio broadcasts similar to the Indianapolis 500. Air shows and various events became a mainstay until the Speedway was ultimately carved up to make way for new development.

The success, high profile, and oil riches of the city did not escape the notice of neighboring Los Angeles in 1923. Coveting the water and image of the small city, Los Angeles proposed annexation, but famous residents like Pickford and Rogers vehemently opposed the measure and amassed support among the residents. Although some believed it was a sound idea that would provide more water for growth, the proposal was defeated. The battle to become an independent city fueled the little metropolis's political conscience and Hollywood's liberal mentality never disappeared from the lush landscape.

As the city gained in power and prestige, hotels like the Beverly-Wilshire Hotel arrived and high-profile mansions like Greystone, built by Edward "Ned" L. Doheny, Jr., the only son and heir of oil magnate Edward L. Doheny, fueled Beverly Hills' elegant reputation. Originally part of the largest family estate in the history of Beverly Hills, Greystone remains a treasured landmark and the site of the mysterious and infamous unsolved murder of Ned Doheny. Completed in 1928 at a cost of $3,166,780, the mansion was home to Ned, his wife Lucy, and their five children. The expansive 46,000-square-foot estate included 55 rooms, tennis courts, a swimming pool, a green house, a fire station, and kennels. After a series of sales, the mansion was purchased by the City of Beverly Hills in 1965 and formally dedicated as a public park in 1971. In 1976, Greystone Mansion was recognized as a historic landmark and placed on the National Register of Historic Places. Today it is a symbol of how the glamour of Hollywood and the wealth of oil met and bonded within the borders of Beverly Hills.

From the early wildcatters to the power of oil magnates like Edward Doheny, oil has been a part of Beverly Hills life since the beginning. Today, wells exist beneath scores of Beverly Hills homes and royalties are paid throughout the year to the families who own the land through which the black gold is pumped. Oil has always been a fact of life for the city and its inhabitants, and both entities managed to coexist in peaceful serenity.

That is until that fateful day in November 2002 when Erin Brockovich came to town and added a new chapter to the city's illustrious history. Suddenly, residents who had little acquaintance with oil other than their cars or a royalty check for the slant drilling beneath their homes were faced with a new kind of check—a reality one. But oil and Beverly Hills were not soon to part ways, despite the attempts of lawyers to tear them asunder.

9

Shouldering the Burden

Insurance—an ingenious modern game of chance in which the player is permitted to enjoy the comfortable conviction that he is beating the man who keeps the table.

—Ambrose Bierce

With the entrance of Erin Brockovich and her claims, the peaceful coexistence between Beverly Hills and oil shattered. The long-standing acceptance of the numerous wells beneath scores of Beverly Hills homes had been transformed to fear, anger, and frustration, all magnified by one insufficiently answered question: the veracity of Brockovich's allegations concerning the chemical levels of her original test results. Since the city and school district did not believe they had been presented with all the necessary papers concerning Erin's results, and their requests continued to go unanswered, they were forced to subpoena the information.

Ultimately, the courts were forced to intervene and restore calm as the Masry & Vititoe law firm answered the City of Beverly Hills' legislative subpoena with a one-two punch by filing another 74 claims and taking dead aim at the oil companies with a giant arrow. In papers filed in Los Angeles Superior Court on June 9, 2003, the firm alleged, among other things, negligence, malice and oppression, strict liability, fraudulent concealment, intentional infliction of emotional distress, negligent infliction of emotional distress, battery, alter ego/piercing the corporate veil, single enterprise, loss of consortium, survival action, and wrongful death.

Lawsuits cost money, and most school districts have a sorry shortage of that commodity. To battle Brockovich, the district would need millions to cover court costs and attorneys' fees. Add to that the exorbitant testing bills and the total would be a hefty amount for any school system to incur.

Although the Beverly Hills School Board legally was the landlord on Venoco's lease, the city was heavily involved as a signatory because of the millions they give to the schools each year under their joint powers agreement. As claims mounted, the city council offered to take the lead in litigation over the oil wells in an effort to reduce the cost to the school board. In a letter sent to the board on July 29 by the council, the city offered to incur the greater part of the fees to lessen duplicative expenses. Since Ed Masry's February 6 announcement of his intention to sue, the district had incurred legal fees of over $300,000. Thus, it had cost the district approximately $50,000 a month to defend itself against Brockovich's allegations.

Then-mayor Tom Levyn commented, "My fellow councilmembers [Mark Egerman, Steve Webb, Linda Briskman, Jimmy Delshad] and I enjoy our relationship with the school board and superintendent. Enhancing our children's education, improving curriculum and developing intellectually curious students is a continuing challenge, with opportunities for success directly linked to the amount of accessible resources.

"The city council believes the school district's budget is being severely impacted and compromised by the amount of attorney fees and costs incurred in litigation and has made a written offer to the school board which would substantially reduce the district's reliance on outside lawyers. Now that the lawsuit has been filed, as a group Mark, Steve, Linda, Jimmy and I submitted our proposal in the hope the school board would quickly accept it, or at least hold a special meeting to consider the merits. The goal of the city council is to preserve programs and teachers.

"Each day that goes by means more attorney fees and costs building up against the school district's limited resources, which the council believes is easily avoidable."

In the letter stating their offer, the council told the school board,

> We are writing you on behalf of the entire city council because of the economic damage currently caused by the lawsuits filed by the law firms of Masry/Vititoe and Baron and Budd against the district and the city in connection with the oil facilities located on district property. Budget limitations of the district have been imposed upon you by economic circumstance, not by your personal or professional choice. No one desires to see teachers or programs of the district cut or reduced in scope, which can only have a dramatic negative impact on the reputation of Beverly Hills' schools.

The council went on to explain their reasons for the offer:

> Further, no one desires to see school board members or our superintendent expend the better part of their energies and intellectual capital on litigation strategies and related attorneys' fees and costs when there is an alternative that is less intrusive and less expensive.
>
> As your colleagues and friends, and with knowledge of the challenging task you undertake daily to educate the children of the Beverly Hills Unified School District, we believe the city can be of aid in substantially reducing your litigation expenses. This would allow you to use limited economic

resources for educational purposes and not for defending the district in costly lawsuits.

As you know, both the district and the city have employed litigation counsel and insurance coverage counsel to provide advice and guidance in the Masry lawsuit and other oil well-related claims. When both bodies utilize outside lawyers, there is an opportunity for duplication of efforts, which can greatly increase the fees and costs in any lawsuit. The chance to reach economies of scale is considerably and sadly reduced.

Therefore, we again restate our offer to assume the majority of legal costs from this point forward. This offer is made in the hope that our mutual goals may be reached and the district may be released from the iron grip of attorney fees and costs. Further, as you are aware, even if an insurance company agrees to pay for the costs of defending the district with independent counsel, insurance companies typically will reimburse attorney fees at rates substantially below those charged by law firms practicing in this area.

The letter continued with a summary of what the city was proposing, including the option to terminate the agreement:

Either the city or the district would have the right to terminate the above relationship at any time and for any reason, or for no reason, upon ten days' written notice, which leaves the district free to select another option if it chooses to do so.

We strongly urge you to consider our offer and to accept it immediately, thereby saving needed funds for the future of education in Beverly Hills. If the district accepts this offer, we will immediately instruct counsel to make the appropriate arrangements.

Mark Egerman, the vice mayor, noted that the board would retain some legal expenses with their own counsel, but there would be far less duplication. "There is not a lot of downside for the city and there is a large upside to the district. They will still need some legal counsel, but it will be far less this way. It will also help to avoid future budget cuts."

He believed the city was better equipped financially to shoulder the burden of the mounting legal costs of the district. "It seems unnecessary for duplicative legal fees in this case," Egerman said. "Both of us are basically doing the same work and just like the city paid for the CDM testing, we feel we should also be helping to pay the legal fees. This would allow the board to address their educational issues with less distractions."

Barry Brucker, school board president, responded to the letter. "I was personally handed the proposal Tuesday, July 29. Our closed board meeting was that afternoon where all board members were given copies. With critical decisions to be made regarding Dr. Gross's resignation, the board did not have adequate time to review and discuss the proposal. With members on vacation, any further discussion regarding such a proposal will have to wait until we can meet as a whole. It would be inappropriate to comment any further on the nature of this proposal."

When the proposal was ultimately reviewed by the board, the members did not agree with the city's assumptions. In actuality, the city received quite the opposite response its councilmembers anticipated. Brucker commented at the time that he was not inclined to agree that both the city and the school board's interests would be served from joining together. In fact, the board members were hesitant to relinquish control to the city and believed it counterproductive to the board's interests. There was a definite "thanks, but no thanks" attitude apparent in their demeanor. After checking thoroughly to ascertain their insurance companies would cover costs, the school board declined the offer.

Instead, the district would rely on its defense and indemnity insurance to pay for legal costs. A statement issued by the district read, "The school district is vigorously defending itself against these lawsuits and there is a mountain of scientific evidence showing there is no health risk at the high school site. The district would rather spend taxpayers' dollars in the classroom than in the courtroom. That is why the district has insurance coverage." However, only a short time after the board members declined the city's financial support, a number of the Beverly Hills School Board's insurance carriers refused to respond to the district's claim requests. As legal bills related to the Brockovich/Masry lawsuit escalated over the $1 million mark, ongoing insurance concerns forced the school district to ensure coverage by alternative carriers while they brought the delinquent carriers to court. Legal bills continued to mount as the school district and city prepared their defenses.

According to the school board's original attorney, David Orbach, one of the interesting financial aspects of the suit against the insurance companies was that a group of carriers simply ignored the district's tender of its defense/indemnity claim, neither rejecting or accepting the claim, despite their obligations to respond under California law. When contacted, the carriers declined to comment on allegations they were in violation of California Code of Regulations, title 10, chapter 5, sections 2695.5 and 2695.7 (a). The code specifies, "Upon receiving any written or oral inquiry from the Department of Insurance concerning a claim, every licensee shall immediately, but in no event more than twenty-one (21) calendar days of receipt of that inquiry, furnish the Department of Insurance with a complete written response based on the facts as then known by the licensee." It goes on to state, "Upon receiving proof of claim, every insurer, except as specified in subsection 2695.7(e)(4) below, shall immediately, but in no event more than forty (40) calendar days later, accept or deny the claim, in whole or in part." Section 2695.7 (1) states, "Where an insurer denies or rejects a first party claim, in whole or in part, it shall do so in writing and shall provide to the claimant a statement listing all bases for such rejection or denial and the factual and legal bases for each reason given for such rejection or denial which is then within the insurer's knowledge."

The carriers totaled $23.8 million in liability coverage. It took the district over a year to track down and establish the carriers throughout the over twenty years named in its suit. Among the carriers mentioned in the suit were New Hampshire Insurance Company, Heath Urban National Union Fire Insurance Company, Highlands Insurance Company, Gulf Insurance Company, and Lloyd's of London. Orbach said Gulf Insurance denied the district's tender even though it is owned by Travelers, which along with Balboa, accepted the district's defense. Gulf has the same policy language as Travelers, which makes denial by Gulf even more arbitrary. He accused the insurers of either refusing to acknowledge their duty to defend the lawsuits or of denying coverage, forcing the school to pay its own legal costs. The lawsuit asked the court to declare that each of the insurers had a duty to defend Beverly Hills High School and asked for unspecified damages.

"This is especially puzzling since Gulf Insurance, who is named in the lawsuit, comes under the umbrella of Travelers, which has allowed coverage of the suit," Barry Brucker said. "I just don't understand how they can refuse to respond to us when it's the law, and I'm curious to see how they will explain this to a judge."

Wainoco Oil, the oil company preceding Venoco Oil at Beverly Hills High School, was also embroiled in a legal battle with Royal and Sun Alliance Insurance of Canada, fighting to have the case heard in the Canadian courts. Wainoco was insured with Royal for $3.5 million from 1988 to 1990.

According to a spokesman for the district, there are several issues involving insurance coverage and two obligations: the first, the duty to defend a potential case and the other, to indemnify. The courts view these differently. The duty to defend comes into play simply if there is a potential litigation. Then the coverage would extend to defense. Indemnification would address potential loss through litigation. The spokesman explained that with progressive loss such as mold or asbestos cases, rather than say a sudden and immediate one—perhaps an auto accident—the insurers adjust their payouts according to a percentage of responsibility time carried. When there are potentially overlapping responsibilities among insurance companies, the companies divide the costs through formulation.

There was also a battle with insurance companies over what was termed the "pollution exclusion." An argument was made that the insurance carrier was not responsible for an illness or injury caused by pollution, but a school district spokesman verified that some of the policies predated the pollution exclusion addition. When there is a dispute over coverage in the state of California, it is given to the courts to decide how to resolve that contract dispute.

Insurance companies have a large impact on the decision of the defendant to continue fighting a lawsuit, and it was becoming clear that expenses would be astronomical despite the outcome of the Brockovich case. These companies consider the bottom line. So, for example, if the cost of fighting Brockovich and Masry becomes far greater than say, paying them to go away, the decision is in the hands of the insurance carriers. This may prove to be a happy ending for the lawyers who are faced with years of legal battles or a weak case and may ultimately lose and wind up with no money at all. Quite simply, no one was anxious to furnish payouts if it was at all possible to avoid doing so. At the end of the day, however, after more legal wrangling, the insurance companies ultimately paid the bills.

While the details of who was picking up the check were being decided, Erin was continuing her interviews and allegations in the public forum. As Venoco production at BHHS increased to four hundred barrels a day in the summer of 2003, Erin appeared on the *Today* show and raised allegations that the city was intentionally keeping the Department of Toxic Substances Control (DTSC) away from the site. She also claimed the AQMD was refusing to furnish Baron and Budd with data on former inspections. She stated, "The South Coast Air Quality Management District is not releasing some of the test results that they have, in fact, found."

AQMD spokesman Sam Atwood responded to Brockovich's allegation, noting, "The AQMD has always provided the public with all the information relating to Venoco and air quality at BHHS and we will continue to do so in the future. Specifically, we issued a series of memos to all interested parties, concerned parents and the school district, who posted the information on the school's website." The school district also began posting my articles on the their website regularly as a way of updating parents on new information.

On the *Today* show, Erin also referred to a memo dated February 11, 2003, that alluded to the level of benzene sampled in the vent pipe of the Venoco facility and reported it at 2.1 parts per million. However, she did not note that once the amine unit was replaced the numbers returned to normal levels.

Brockovich insisted she and her legal team were "not going to be comfortable with anything until the school district allows the appropriate agency—which is the Department of Toxic Substances and Control—on to that site . . . and this is a school that has eighteen operational oil heads and a natural gas processing facility underneath it. This agency needs to be allowed on-site to do risk assessments to ensure that these kids are, in fact, safe."

City Attorney Larry Wiener and Hamid Saebfar, director of the DTSC, addressed Erin's comments. Wiener insisted that the DTSC was allowed access: "We invited the DTSC to participate, but they wouldn't unless we followed all their procedures. We didn't believe that we could obtain the results from all the testing before school started if we had followed the DTSC process. Therefore, we used the DTSC protocol for testing and moved forward on our own."

Saebfar agreed with Wiener and added that the DTSC had toured the site, including the Venoco facility. "Chris Bisgaard, attorney for the city, contacted us and wanted us to be involved because we do environmental assessment at new school sites," Saebfar told me. "He wanted us to evaluate the high school and see if there was any potential health threat on the property or coming from the oil well. We got together and developed a contract based on our fee for service; we work on a fee basis and there is no state money for our service. We said we would oversee the investigation at BHHS. Later on, I was told that the school district and the city were not willing to sign. They wanted to do limited investigations and the DTSC wanted to check for every potential dangerous hazardous contaminant. But the city and school district said we were welcome to oversee the investigation." Saebfar chose not to accept without a contract, noting that unless work proceeded according to their work plan and was implemented with their oversight, it would be difficult to determine safety. "We're not saying there is a problem or anyone is trying to hide something, we really don't know."

Wiener said the city filed a complaint alleging Masry's original complaint was inadequate in several ways—including failing to provide specifics—and Masry chose to amend his complaint instead of refiling.

As the legal posturing continued, so too did the public relations blitz. Brockovich told the *Today* show that the law firm they were working with—Baron and Budd—"have themselves hired very competent experts who are looking at all the data, all the numbers and all of the problems. And what we've done is we've taken all of these Hodgkin's—let's just take that—and crunched these numbers. And no matter which way you look at it, we'll give them everything they want. This school has four times the national average of Hodgkin's than anywhere else in America."

Venoco vice president Mike Edwards was surprised by Erin's statement. "I was shocked to hear her say there was a cancer cluster, when their own attorneys admitted in court they had never done an epidemiological study," he said.

Mark Katchen of the Phylmar Group, Inc., the district's environmental specialist, released his report on the high school indoor air quality testing that same week in November, 2003. The report summary concluded maximum concentrations of all petroleum production-related VOCs—except for three chemicals—were within the background ranges typically found within the Los Angeles Basin. Katchen said the report showed methane concentrations measured during the third round of sampling were consistent with background levels and far less than the methane lower explosive limit. "Similarly, detected concentrations of propane were well below levels at which it posed an explosive hazard. Therefore," he concluded, "no explosive risk was present."

Although tests appeared to reflect safe conditions, Erin continued to allege otherwise in articles and on television. The following interview with Anderson Cooper on CNN is typical of her public relations efforts. As late as June 15, 2006, she remained adamant it was unsafe and the cause of the cancers, although no definitive or scientific studies of the school population epidemiology had been done.

In the CNN interview, Anderson Cooper alluded to the dangers in downtown Beverly Hills and high school alumna Lori Moss's diagnosis with cancer twice in her twenties. Moss told Cooper she found it difficult to believe she had contracted two cancers at such a young age. When she met Brockovich at a book signing she became convinced it was no coincidence.

Anderson reported that Erin had investigated and come up with a cause for the cancers. Brockovich said she had read an article about the ways in which the oil industry cleverly masks their oil operations. Cooper pointed to the oil derrick on Beverly Hills High School's campus, brightly decorated with flowers painted by terminally ill children and named the Tower of Hope. Brockovich told Cooper, "And then I thought, how could that be? At a public high school? You have basically an onshore oil platform and nobody knows it's there? That's really kind of what initially set me off because nobody had a clue. Nobody knew."

Cooper said, "Brockovich set out to investigate, researching and testing the air quality of the school and hired Columbia Analytical Services, a network of laboratories that specializes in environmental testing. The company found abnormal amounts of toxins in the air admitted from the derrick and the power plant's cooling towers."

It should be noted that in the interview Cooper reports that Columbia Analytical Services found abnormal levels. This is true. However, it is implied that they performed the test, which is incorrect. Erin, Bernard Endres, and Jim Drury, employed by the Masry & Vititoe law firm, did the physical investigation at the school. Columbia read the results delivered to them and would not and could not vouch for where or how the tests were done.

Cooper then reported Brockovich's claims that the oil well toxins had resulted in more than four hundred people, either high school alumnae or residents living near the well, developing cancer. Erin said they filed more than eight hundred lawsuits on behalf of such plaintiffs in 2003.

Beverly Hills city and school officials, although they declined an interview on the program, did issue a release saying, "The safety of our children and all of the children in our community is our highest priority. The school district and the city hired an internationally respected environmental testing firm. That firm was unable to find any unusual conditions at the high school. The state's air pollution control agency, the South Coast Air Quality Management District, found nothing unusual. Even the testing performed under the direction of the plaintiffs' lawyers showed the air quality at the high school is typical for Los Angeles."

Brockovich countered studies showing no link between pollution from oil wells and the types of cancers the lawsuit focuses on by saying, "I'm just that ordinary person that tells you common sense is kind of kicking in here for me somewhere. You've got an unusual number of kids, in my humble little opinion, with cancer."

Cooper did add in closing that one cancer epidemiologist contacted by CNN said that certain types of cancers are appearing more frequently in the young adult population nationwide, but the trend is largely attributed to improved diagnostic techniques.

Barry Brucker insists although these half truths may seem like a small thing, it is these muddy and unchallenged statements and allegations, that allow these types of lawsuits to progress through the courts for years. When questioned about Brockovich's comments on the *Today Show,* Brucker remarked, "My only concern is whether Beverly High is safe. You could be certain that I wouldn't be sending my daughter there if I didn't feel confident in the consistent positive test results."

10

Benzene-Laced Legalese

Beware of the prophet seeking profits.

—Dennis Miller

Week after week as new skirmishes were fought in the war of words, the news stories addressed various battlefronts. While the City of Beverly Hills sought to acquire Masry's data, the AQMD was having its own problems pursuing an agreement with Venoco over the amine unit permit. Ed Masry continued to insist that students at BHHS were at risk and should be undergoing medical monitoring. He also claimed the Venoco health risk assessment ordered by the AQMD would only be valid if done by a reputable company.

My conversations with Ed Masry varied constantly. I actually enjoyed his blustering tone and found it amusing, although for many weeks it was directed personally at me. Whenever a story of mine appeared with facts casting doubt on his claims he would say, "You are the worst journalist I have ever seen" and slam down the phone. When he had something to offer that bolstered his case, he would take the time to explain it carefully in his oft-colorful and highly dramatic manner. "Some companies could be in the middle of an anthrax epidemic and say all is well," Masry said once. "I think what the schools and the AQMD are doing is atrocious. People better know that they better start medical monitoring early if they want to survive."

Masry claimed his readings showed the volatile organic compounds at the high school were five times higher than levels at the 405 Freeway. At that time he had over 700 clients, 460 of whom had cancer; the remainder were suing for medical monitoring.

Many of the legal disputes concerned who gave what information to whom and what some party was withholding. "We just filed a subpoena against the AQMD because they refuse to give us their records. You are going to find when the truth comes out that there are huge readings of benzene. They have to give us those records under the Freedom of Information Act, but they just don't want to reveal to the public what the real numbers are," Masry told me.

Dr. Barry Wallerstein, executive director of the AQMD, responded to Masry's claims that they were withholding information: "The only records we couldn't provide are ones we are forbidden under the law to release to anyone, because they may give a competitor an unfair advantage. All other test results and records have been released to anyone who has requested them."

According to AQMD legal counsel Kurt Wiese, Masry's request was too vast to be answered in the amount of time allotted. "We were served in September and the subpoena contained a 62-page document. In that document were listed 26 companies and under each company there were 26 questions regarding documents relating to that company.

"We contacted the plaintiff's attorney and didn't hear back for quite a while. I was contacted by Baron and Budd in

Texas and discussed a proposal with them concerning more time. He said they couldn't make the decision but would let me know. When he called back he said his co-counsel was unwilling to discuss additional time and wanted the response by the twenty-fifth of September."

Wiese drafted a motion to either free them from answering the motion or give them more time to respond. Judge Wendell Mortimer of Los Angeles Superior Court, Central Division, set a hearing for the AQMD to comply with the subpoena of their records. Wiese hoped the judge would then address the AQMD motion because he claimed the request was overwhelming. "We are more than happy to turn over the records. But when you get served with a 62-page subpoena, you need time."

As Wiese would explain to the judge, his efforts to convince Baron and Budd to extend the time period were repudiated. "The real amazing part is they won't talk to us about arranging a reasonable schedule," he said. He reiterated his intention, saying any new motion to order AQMD compliance was unnecessary as they planned to fulfill the request. He stated, "We are hoping by the December 12 hearing date we will be able to furnish them with the bulk of the information." He explained part of the problem was the necessity to establish whether or not the requested information actually exists.

Wallerstein confirmed that Masry's request was difficult because records petitioned predated the existence of the current AQMD. "Many of those records are off site and we have to search through and see if they even exist. Then, each record must be read to ensure that nothing is released which is proprietary information and against the law to release." A request of that magnitude would force the AQMD to shut down most of its operations to seek out the material, which Wallerstein insisted was not possible.

Wallerstein went on to say that they had examined emissions from the Sempra site near BHHS and done a health risk assessment. They did not believe that that facility would account for Masry's reported measurements or findings. In fact, all testing done at the site continued to show numbers within normal ranges, but the city had committed to ongoing testing and monitoring to ensure health safety.

During that time radon gas testing results were returned, again confirming normal levels at the high school and surrounding areas. Kathleen Kaufman, L.A. County Department of Public Health Radiation Management director, said radon tests results showed acceptable levels. "No readings even approaching the Environmental Protection Agency's action levels were found."

As all fears, claims, and counterclaims flew through the supposedly toxic Beverly Hills air, Venoco issued an official statement in response to the Masry lawsuit:

> A group of 21 plaintiffs filed a lawsuit alleging they had contracted Hodgkin's lymphoma as a result of oil production operations located in Beverly Hills, California. Venoco, Inc. was named as a defendant by one of the 21 plaintiffs in the lawsuit, which was filed in Los Angeles County Superior Court. The allegations directed at Venoco are false and Venoco will defend itself vigorously.
>
> Testing and analysis conducted by the South Coast Air Quality Management District, which is the governmental agency responsible for air quality, has concluded that Venoco's operations are safe. Following initial allegations by the plaintiffs' attorneys about air quality at Beverly Hills High School, the Air Quality Management District conducted extensive tests. Over a 3-month period, the Air Quality Management District tested the air quality on six different

days, compiling more than 40 hours of air sampling. The Air Quality Management District tested the air at several locations each time, including locations on the high school grounds and on Venoco's production site. The tests were conducted on days when Venoco was conducting normal oil and natural gas production operations, as well as on days when production was completely halted. According to the most recent Air Quality Management District memorandum characterizing the test results, "Monitoring at the high school area has not shown readings of benzene, hexane, and other air toxic levels that are considered abnormal. In addition, the measured level of propane and ethane in the samples are not considered a threat to human health."

The City of Beverly Hills also hired an independent testing firm to conduct additional air quality tests, which were performed while Venoco was in normal production. Those tests reached the same conclusion as the Air Quality Management District, that air quality at Beverly Hills High School was normal.

The Venoco production site occupies eight thousand square feet. No refining occurs on the site. The oil is transmitted by pipeline to a refinery in Long Beach and the natural gas is transmitted by pipeline to the gas company for local distribution. Contrary to the plaintiffs' allegations, there are no abandoned wells on the Venoco site. There are, however, underground wells on other parts of the school field that are remnants from previous oil leases with other oil companies.

Aside from Venoco, others mentioned in the lawsuit were Wainoco (from whom Venoco purchased the site), Frontier Oil, Waverly Oil, Arco Petroleum, Beverly Hills Oil (Chevron), Gulf Standard Oil (Texaco), and Sempra. These companies either presently operated or had once operated wells or facilities on the field. In the lawsuit, Masry alleged, "This case is about the inexcusable and knowing failure of the oil and gas industry and municipal and administrative bodies to protect school children, the most vulnerable in society, at the places that should be most safe . . . schools."

Among those named in the suit as plaintiffs were Lori Lynn Moss and Randy Moss, Timothy Alden Ross, Lori Urov (deceased), Autumn Isabelle Haagen, Mark Lewis Adelman, William David Gooch, and Lone S. Gooch, Andrew Ball and Karen Ball, Gary Aaron Davidson, Steven Homer Kreitenberg, Kelli Grant, Allison Patricia Levy, Carl Benton Wilson, Howard Jay Sapper, and Michael Isaac Zielinski.

The case was assigned to Superior Court judge William Highberger. As soon as the suit was filed I attempted to call Brockovich and Masry for comment and was told they had hired a high-profile Beverly Hills public relations firm; the PR firm refused a request for a statement or to return my phone calls.

Despite Masry & Vititoe/Baron and Budd attorney Rick Ottaiano's attempts to explain away their admission that they had done no epidemiological study, Los Angeles Superior Court judge Valerie Baker ordered the Masry firm to turn over documentation of the firm's testing and raw data by noon on July 22 to comply with the legislative subpoena. The city's request for Masry's testing results was countered by claims the information was work product and came under the heading of privilege. The judge disagreed and it seemed the city was finally going to get a look at the data they had been seeking.

Beverly Hills city attorney Larry Wiener explained that Masry would now have to turn over all the necessary documents ordered by the court or face contempt and possibly even jail. Wiener said the admission that there had been no study should provide parents with a sense of safety about the school environment. He explained, "It seems that the only evidence regarding the health and safety at Beverly Hills High School is evidence developed by the AQMD, the city and the school district, which shows that it is safe for students to attend BHHS."

Skip Miller, outside counsel for the city and proponent for the use of the legislative subpoenas, saw the judge's ruling as a very positive result for the city. "This ruling essentially means that Masry & Vititoe and Baron and Budd have been put to the test and they are coming up empty."

On the advice of their attorneys, one of Masry's testing labs, Columbia Analytical Services in Simi Valley, showed up in court with all their raw data in order to comply with the city's subpoenas.

Masry & Vititoe's Jim Drury, who did the initial testing for the firm, reacted strongly to the day's events. "They are just harassing us and it's going to end up backfiring on them in a big way when this goes to trial." Drury said the problem with the testing is that it is just a "photograph" of what is happening on one day. "Why is the facility turned off? Because there are huge problems over there. It's leaking all over the place and it's a filthy operation," Drury insisted.

When asked if the Masry firm was going to do a study, Drury said they had not done one and did not plan to undertake one. "How can I do a study when they throw me off the campus every time I go there? Every time I step foot on campus someone tries to put me in jail."

Drury went on to say that it is the city's responsibility to undertake that level of study and protect the students. "Why do we have four hundred alumni and staff members with cancer?" he asked. "Because there's bad air in L.A.? I don't think so. This is criminal. There is an exposure pathway there and they don't want to find it and I haven't been given an opportunity. We opened our arms to the city and the school district and I was in the process of getting them the data and they subpoenaed me. This is harassment, but finding out why, when, and what really happened to those people is what's important and I'm leaving the other stuff up to the lawyers."

These stories were the weekly diet of benzene-laced legalese the city was fed. I often had numerous updates to address in a single story and there was always something new to report. But although the case was still unfolding, I admit, many days I wondered how many residents aside from Jody Kleinman were still paying attention.

Aside from gleaning truth from a maze of facts, one challenge in presenting weekly updates on the lawsuit was ensuring interesting reading. Disseminating information was useless if no one in the city was paying attention, so cutting through the sludge of long, boring lists of chemicals and court proceedings often proved a daunting task.

Beverly Hills is a highly educated community and quite adept at comprehending complex issues. This double-edged sword proved good and bad as many derived great satisfaction in spotting typos and errors in the paper and calling me out on them. Fridays, after the paper had been delivered, I would receive phone calls about a misplaced comma in a caption on page 56 or a misspelled word on page 28. I would also be derided for giving one community member more quotes in an article than another or placing someone's picture farther back in the paper, but I found it amusing and it kept me on my toes.

Most of what went on in the courtroom were long, tedious monologues by the attorneys. I once asked how opposing counsels could be so civil when it was apparent they were out for blood. In answer, I received the old cliché: nothing personal, just doing my job. That didn't ring true in this case—especially when hundreds of millions of dollars were the golden carrot on the stick. On a typical day in court, the intensity in the courtroom teemed with an undercurrent of urgency, despite the civil demeanor of the opposing counsels. I imagine it's a lawyer thing, because I never sensed a separation between emotion and intent.

Unable to be present at every court date throughout the seven-year span, I often relied on an update from Beverly Hills city attorney Larry Wiener or looked over the court documents. I couldn't always afford to leave the paper for half a day, as many of the appearances were simply to set another date for motions. At times the court would convene for half an hour, at times longer, according to the business addressed that day. Each court appearance would garner new judgments and rulings, and judges' decisions were frequently made immediately, but there were times when the issue was taken under advisement and ruled on at another appearance.

As the rulings proceeded, Judge Mortimer denied the defendants' demurrer request, a court request that a lawsuit be dismissed because it has no legal claim. The city's attorneys had asked that plaintiffs provide more information before proceeding with their case. The defendants asked for thirty days to respond to the judge's ruling instead of the fifteen the judge originally requested, and Mortimer concurred.

Among the other issues that arose during the many court dates was the causal relationship between the chemicals and the diseases. Attorney Deanna Miller for Sempra Energy told the court the complaint provided a laundry list of chemicals and she believed the plaintiffs should tie the diseases to the chemicals in a more specific manner. In other words, they needed to clarify which chemicals are alleged to cause which illnesses. Mortimer denied her request and gave them thirty days to answer his ruling.

The judge asked whether attorneys felt the court should set another status conference, but Chevron's attorney said they were working hard to comply with plaintiffs' requests for documents and should be able to deliver them in a timely fashion. Baron and Budd attorney Al Stewart agreed that the time frame for delivery of documentation could be accomplished without the need for further court intervention. A court date was set for July 25, 2005, to begin hearing the case, and Stewart said he was confident he would have all the necessary documentation for the jury. "I don't believe in trying my cases in the press. Just wait until next July when all the facts are presented to the jury." I heard this mantra countless times from Stewart and yet, every time I turned around, Erin was discussing the issue in a different article or television interview.

I remember one of the first court appearances and how taken I was with the vast sea of lawyers spread throughout the courtroom. I was quite out of my element but very intrigued. Armed with notepads and briefcases containing reams of ammunition, a sea of warriors dressed in Brooks Brothers suits and striped ties converged on the Los Angeles Superior Courthouse to do battle. Had a jury been selected, there wouldn't have been room to seat them that day. All seats were filled with stern Ivy League grads with Marine-issue buzz haircuts; the warrior look seemed quite appropriate for the battle about to commence. It was obvious no prisoners would be taken. This was an intimidating crew of attorneys by anyone's standards.

Lawyers sized up their opponents and calculated strategies

as notes were scribbled at a fast and furious pace. The tone was subdued, yet charged with determination. Attorney Chris Bisgaard, of Lewis, Brisbois, Bisgaard & Smith, led the city's defense team with Skip Miller of Christensen, Miller, Fink, Jacobs, Glaser, Weil & Shapiro alongside. Baron and Budd mounted their horses with Allen M. Stewart and James D. Piel leading the charge.

Bisgaard adopted the mantra, "There's no there, there," and repeated it often and with mounting conviction as the case progressed. Following disagreements over discovery, Stewart stated his objections over what he believed was the city's unfair advantage through the issuance of their legislative subpoenas. Skip Miller answered Stewart's complaint, explaining to the court the need to invoke legislative powers. "The legislative proceedings were initiated after plaintiffs' attorneys went to the press and indicated there were air quality problems," Miller stated. "For obvious reasons, the city has the jurisdictional authority to determine whether or not there is a current problem and it was a great relief to find there were no issues with the air."

Stewart responded that he was not aware that an "all clear" had been sounded regarding the health risks posed by the well nor that the city was alone in the right to conduct discovery. The plaintiffs' attorney told Judge Mortimer that he was in the position of having to prove his case without receiving necessary court documents. Bisgaard countered that it would be inappropriate for plaintiffs to file a complaint based on evidence and then try to develop that evidence in a "fishing expedition."

The plaintiffs' team had also claimed that certain questions on a 1978 Environmental Impact Report contained a "maybe" answer in response to potential site dangers. Brockovich said these answers had not been followed up or properly addressed. The city's attorney Skip Miller sited the 1984 Environmental Impact Report for the oil site, insisting their claims were highly misleading. "The accusations regarding the EIR are unfounded," Miller told the court. "They point to information which is relevant to the construction of the well, not the well itself. The key element in the EIR is section II 21, (d), which asks: Does the project have environmental effects which will cause substantial adverse effects on human beings, either directly or indirectly? The answer checked is 'no.'"

Regarding the legislative subpoenas, Bisgaard told Judge Mortimer that "the city was anxious to get the case resolved as soon as possible and they believed they had the mechanism to do that." Stewart requested the judge issue a discovery protection order and the judge asked if Bisgaard would agree. Bisgaard agreed to the order if it was bilateral (meaning both parties would be held equally accountable). Stewart agreed to redraft his request as a bilateral order.

Stewart then asked Judge Mortimer to consider hearing *Moss v. Venoco* first, although the case dealt primarily with Hodgkin's lymphoma and non-Hodgkin's lymphoma cases. Bisgaard objected vehemently on the grounds that Moss was not a widely representative sampling of the cancers named in the over seven hundred lawsuits filed thus far. When asked why he had pursued this avenue, Stewart answered, "The Moss claim was filed first and it is a time-honored rule that cases first filed should be tried first." He noted that because there are fewer issues in the Moss complaint, it could be resolved sooner than complaints that may have one hundred plaintiffs.

Bisgaard argued that addressing a case not widely representative would prove counterproductive and costly. "We think proceeding with Moss first is exactly the wrong thing to do here. We think the first group should typify a wider cross-section and we would propose consolidation. That would enable us to learn from the verdict and indicate whether or not there is reason to move forward."

Judge Mortimer subsequently ruled that opposing sides could each select six plaintiffs as a representative sampling for the jury trial. The following plaintiffs were selected:

Janet Lee Day, born 11/12/66, attended Beverly from 1980 to 1984, suffers from Hodgkin's lymphoma and thyroid cancer

Linnea M. Shore, 11/10/61, attended Beverly from 1975 to 1979, suffers from non-Hodgkin's lymphoma

John Laurie, 2/26/62, never attended Beverly, suffers from thyroid cancer

Melissa Beth Gross, 2/5/70, attended Beverly from 1984 to 1988, suffers from breast cancer

Monica Robin Revel, 7/17/75, attended Beverly from 1989 to 1993, suffers from malignant melanoma

Jeffrey Bryan Frankel, 11/1/71, attended Beverly from 1985 to 1989, suffers from testicular cancer

Gary Aaron Davidson, 3/22/64, attended Beverly from 1978 to 1982, suffers from Hodgkin's lymphoma

Stace Tackaberry, 2/22/42, attended Beverly from 1956 to 1960, suffers from non-Hodgkin's lymphoma

Jaimie M. Shapiro, 6/4/59, attended Beverly from 1973 to 1977, suffers from thyroid cancer

Karen Lee Kalcheim, 9/8/47, attended Beverly from 1961 to 1965, suffers from breast cancer

Christine Busch, 8/4/45, never attended Beverly, suffers from skin cancer

Richard S. Gordon, 7/22/64, attended Beverly from 1978 to 1982, suffers from testicular cancer

Thus would proceed many of the days spent in legal battle. The only addition to the posturing and pleas would be the testimony of the occasional "expert" witness.

11

The Senate Hearing

If we all worked on the assumption that what is accepted as
true is really true, there would be little hope of advance.
— Orville Wright

Although I have quoted the participants and reported the
facts of the lawsuit, I believe there is something highly effective
in reading someone's actual testimony. In debating how best
to accurately describe the point of view of each party, I came
upon the transcript from the Joint Informational Hearing of
the Senate Committee on Health and Human Services. On
March 12, 2004, the California senatorial committee came
together for a hearing on "State and Local Governments' Role
in Preventing and Mitigating Environmental Health Risks in
California Schools." The hearing presented an opportunity
for all sides to express their position on the issues. Despite
a lack of conclusions or any positive changes effected by the
hearing, it affords insight into the political nature inherent in
health policy decisions, which became highly relevant when
Beverly Hills became the centerpiece and guest of honor at
the party. I have selected passages to highlight each person's
position, but the entire transcript is available through the

California State Senate's Health Committee for those who wish a more comprehensive examination of the details.

Chairing the hearing was Deborah Ortiz, state senator, and comprising the panel were Senators Sheila Kuehl, Sam Aanestad, Martha Escutia, Richard Alarcón, and Vice Mayor Mark Egerman of Beverly Hills. Participants were limited to ten minutes, with the exception of Erin Brockovich's experts, who received twenty.

Ortiz opened by explaining that the mission of the hearing would be twofold: an inquiry into potential exposure to toxic substances at Beverly Hills High School and the state and local governments' role in preventing and mitigating environmental health risks at schools across the state. Ortiz noted the committee's intention was not to arrive at any conclusions concerning the outstanding litigation but rather to look at the overarching policy questions inherent in the lawsuit and consider potential statewide implications.

Several policy questions would be addressed, including the state's role when potential health risks arise on school campuses in California. Should the state take on a greater role through the schools' programs within the Department of Toxic Substances Control? The members would also hear details concerning current California law stating that, in the case of air quality violations, the regulatory and enforcement agencies can only pursue either criminal or civil penalties, while in the cases of water protection or soil contamination violations, both enforcement means are available.

Three key questions would be asked of attending regulatory agencies. When did you become aware that there were concerns about potential health risks at Beverly Hills High? What did you do in response to these concerns and what are your legal obligations in such a situation? Do you believe you've fulfilled those obligations?

The first panel member to address the committee was Sen. Sam Aanestad, who focused on the process the Beverly Hills community had taken to resolve the health concerns. He stated, "The school district, the city of Beverly Hills, the county, and the state have spent the last year investigating and reporting on all of these claims, and I'm very interested in learning about their findings and what we've learned from this situation in the last year." Addressing Beverly Hills' situation, Aanestad said, "As a health professional, I have to say that I have to rely on scientific data, and I've studied the testing procedures and the results, so far, that I've seen—as many of the results of the tests that I can obtain—and quite frankly, I'm kind of curious as to how we got this far to begin with." He stated his intention to determine firsthand from personal experience whether or not the claims had merit.

He took a swipe at the media that had exploited the story. "And I'm hoping that the media, who I think in the last year has kind of sensationalized this quite a bit and not reported quite fully in the reports that I read up in Northern California, will do a fair job today in reporting to the people of California what happened here."

Sen. Sheila Kuehl voiced her personal take on the issues: "I'm here to hear what everyone has to say. I may disagree a little bit with my colleague about the difference between scientific and anecdotal evidence, having spent a great deal of time in various movements in which the only way anything came to light was when people told their stories because no one believed them until then. . . .

"We are not here to litigate the case, and therefore, we will not come to a conclusion about who's right and who's wrong.

But the state does play a role in protecting the health of its residents, and in that sense, we want to know whether we're doing an adequate job and whether we need to look at other ways or additional ways in which we may protect, especially, students who are vulnerable going to school."

The next panel member, Vice Mayor Egerman, came out swinging. "When this first allegation was aired on CBS News, the city council and the school board as a team took immediate action to retain CDM to do exhaustive, scientific testing to determine what the state of the high school was. The city literally wrote a blank check for them to design their own testing program without any input from the district or the city to ensure that we would have objective and accurate test results that we could then act on if necessary.

"After a year of testing, I can state that all of the tests done by CDM, AQMD, and the district show that the high school is safe, show that all levels are below the norm, and that we have a safe environment for our children, for our teachers, and for our residents."

Jody Kleinman was the first called to speak and expressed the parents' conundrum. "Parents are caught in the middle; in the middle, on the one hand, of lawyers telling us that our children's high school air was and still might be toxic and causing cancer and, on the other hand, government agencies reassuring us that everything is safe, there's no health risks, and our school has been appropriately investigated.

"Everyone seems so busy defending current and potential lawsuits that valid community concerns have been neglected." Jody accused the agencies of acting "as though they really do have something to hide from us. They've not been held accountable. No one wants a clean bill of health declared for our school, past, present, and future, more than I do. But if problems exist today, let's get it cleaned up. Shame on all of us if we don't." She requested they create an "oversight committee composed of all the relevant regulatory agencies, community and parent representatives, and independent experts selected by the community."

Kleinman told the group that air samplings were not consistent with state and federal guidelines and air monitoring needed to be conducted. "I want you to hold every agency involved in conducting school site assessments responsible for recognizing and adopting state methodology guidelines for assessing new and existing schools. . . . And I want you also to question our city about why we still have no methane gas regulations to protect our schools and community.

"I'm concerned about what exposures they [her two daughters] may have received. The information I've been provided does not give me an estimate or even a clue about past exposures. How can air samples taken only on a limited number of days last year in a limited number of locations possibly address questions about their past exposures ten years ago or even three years ago? They can't."

Kleinman insisted nothing could be resolved without a comprehensive exposure and health risk assessment. "A select and invited group of parents were allowed a few private meetings with city officials and their consultants, but we were not allowed to bring any outside independent experts. Questions went unanswered, and the meetings were terminated."

She vocalized concerns over the Department of Toxic Substances' lack of participation and the city's decision to forego soil tests. Kleinman pointed out the fact that over the last thirty years, the school newspaper had documented offensive industrial odors that they and others could smell on the campus. She and others wanted to know why the city hadn't aggressively pursued these complaints.

Her frustration was apparent and the committee was paying rapt attention to her words. "Parents have spoken at city council and school board meetings expressing fears and concerns. We've called agency after agency seeking help. Over 2,000 signatures have been collected requesting that our city shut down oil and gas production on our campus. We're still waiting for someone to hear us. . . . Elevated chemical concentrations in the air samples have never been adequately explained to us."

She voiced her displeasure at the AQMD for allowing Venoco to self-monitor. "AQMD's own highly publicized, current multimillion-dollar lawsuit against BP ARCO is based on their own admission that oil companies have lied when required to self-report. But AQMD designed a punishment for Venoco that requires us to trust a company that has repeatedly lied to us. Venoco repeatedly said that their equipment was in excellent working order while, at the very same time, they were receiving multiple violation notices for excessive toxic admissions, improper gas venting, poor maintenance, and equipment failures. Who's really being punished here?"

She complained the regulatory agencies apparently display a mindset that protects the interests of the very industries they are supposed to regulate. She singled out the Division of Oil, Gas and Geothermal Resources (DOGGR) and AQMD as having "clearly been deficient in physical inspections and scrutiny of oil and gas facilities. They simply continue a war with each other. No agency seems to have the expertise to oversee all the various regulatory programs associated with air, soil, and water. And I'm not suggesting that any one agency should. At this point, there's no single agency I trust."

Kleinman told the panel she was upset that public

emissions figures contain mistakes; public records are often difficult to obtain, incomplete, and inaccurate; and the report provided by Beverly Hills contains mistakes. Jody had turned to the EPA for explanation. "As one EPA official stated (and I quote), 'No wonder you can't understand this information. It's wrong and meaningless.' If I as a nonscientist am catching all these mistakes, what would somebody objectively and independently analyzing this data find?"

Kleinman believed it was reasonable to ask whether or not industrial facilities should be located at or near school sites. "Common sense tells me that they should not."

Responding to Aanestad's question of whether or not she believed the site to be safe and why her daughter still attended the school, Kleinman said, "I really can't comment scientifically on whether there's risks or not."

Aanestad followed up, "So, the risk to you as a mother can't necessarily be as high as at least going to the point of, 'Hey, I'm taking my kid out of this school.' So, it's more of a concern with you wanting the bureaucracy—the state, the district—to be able to say to you, 'Yes, here's the testing, here's the science, and yes, it's safe.'"

"Have I taken my kid out of the school? No, I haven't yet. Do I think we need to do a better job? Yes," Kleinman responded.

Stephen Williams, a parent at Beverly Hills High who possesses a technical background, spoke next. "I have a Ph.D. in pharmacology from Duke University. I studied environmental toxicology and practiced environmental toxicology at the DuPont Haskell Laboratory for Toxicology and Industrial Medicine. In fact, I set threshold limit values for workers' exposure to chemicals under an industrial hygiene setting. So, I'm a bit familiar with the kinds of testing and the implications for that kind of testing that are done."

Williams noted that he had been involved in reviewing the data over the past year and had reached some conclusions. "First and foremost, I believe that based on the substantial evidence that has been developed—and I think, from my experience, there's a lot of evidence around a body of a school—that the Beverly Hills High School provides a safe physical environment for our son, and the existence of the oil well, as I can see it, poses no additional health risk to him or to any other student or teacher in that school or resident of the community. It's not very pretty, but I don't think it's doing anything deleterious."

He stated his belief that the quality of the air is no different from the air in the rest of the L.A. Basin. "For example, we'd much rather have our child running around on the athletic field and breathing the air there than going into the bathrooms and inhaling side-stream smoke from people who choose to smoke cigarettes there. We would rather have our child running on the athletic field than standing on Olympic Boulevard and breathing auto emissions and micro particles of rubber (asbestos) from break linings and other junk produced by the wear and tear of the thousands of cars that pass this high school every day on Olympic Boulevard and other parts of the city. And in the context of exposure to oil-well-related emissions, all of this might be much preferred to taking our child to visit the La Brea tar pits, for example, which constitute open pools of volatile hydrocarbons. So, I'm just trying to put this in sort of practical reality terms."

Williams cited studies showing evidence that proximity to oil wells and products of refineries do not pose an increased health risk to people who work in them and the many comprehensive epidemiological studies of oil refinery workers, oil rig and platform workers, and gas station attendants have not shown any unusual illnesses specifically or any increases in cancer.

He voiced his content in the numerous studies conducted at the school campus, saying they had allayed his fears and he was comfortable there were no unusual levels of any dangerous chemicals present on or near the school property. Williams also told the members he did not believe there were an "excess of cancers or acute illnesses within a reasonable radius of the school, either among students or long-term residents of the community," adding specifically, "the kinds of cancers that initially were alleged by the kinds of chemicals or that would have been induced by the kinds of chemicals—for example, benzene—are not concentrated in this population, which would be leukemia."

Williams reminded the committee how disturbing it was to him personally that "the legal team that decided to bring the action that will really spark this produced a few spurious results early in some rather clandestine sampling that no experts so far in any forum of open communications, scientific planning, and at significant expense have been able to reproduce, putting us as parents in the rather impossible position of either trying to prove a negative—that is, we're trying to prove that there's zero risk for our kids—or to chase ghosts of toxicity that we're told exist."

Mincing no words, he concluded, "In short, as a resident, parent, and informed scientist, I believe that this is an opportunistic legal scam designed to be maximally sensationalistic with promise of large legal settlements by tickling the most sensitive nerves of what I characterize as a rather liberal, very affluent, child-focused, environmentally conscious community that is by and large not technically savvy and is prone to react radically to the specter of anything that is labeled 'toxic.' Our community was cynically and strategically selected for maximum impact in the media. In fact, there is so laughably little historical or contemporary evidence of anything deleterious, it can be nothing else. I'm sure the screenplay for this one is already being written."

Williams blamed the legal system that permits feeding "the fortunes of the legal vultures to the detriment of the education of our children by raising the unrealistic hope and expectations among a few plaintiffs who are ill and who, of course, will seek remedy any way they can. The crime is this: we, the community, the state, the school board, and students already have lost by engaging, and there's no real way out."

Those were fighting words for Senator Ortiz, who was not about to let those statements go unchallenged, but she allowed her colleagues to question him first. Senator Alarcón asked Williams if any of the studies included teenage statistics. Williams responded that not many teenagers work on oil rigs, but he was aware of reports that focus on the development of teenagers relative to pharmaceuticals, which he said are toxic chemicals, but he was obliged to admit that none of the studies mentioned environmental chemicals specifically.

Kuehl next alluded to Kleinman's previous testimony regarding what she believed to be insufficient testing. "You do feel there's been sufficient testing, and from your point of view, you feel there is no threat to the health of any of the students or staff at the high school."

Williams reiterated, "There's no excess threat versus living anywhere else in the L.A. Basin."

After Kuehl clarified some further points, Senator Escutia asked Dr. Williams about his involvement in the testing. "You were involved in discussions regarding how the data was generated. . . . So, you received no compensation for [your involvement]?"

"No," he answered.

She pointed out that Dr. Williams' Ph.D. was in pharmacology then allowed Ortiz to probe further. "Along that line, you are a headhunter for corporate executives in the scientific community. . . . So, do you place executives in Dow Chemical, Venoco . . .?"

Dr. Williams confirmed that he had indeed placed at major firms such as Dow Chemical, Exxon Oil, and Pfizer, as well as in drug safety and environmental safety.

Ortiz came in for the kill. "And I appreciate your coming. I am absolutely committed to an objective hearing, and that's why you were invited to provide testimony. Ms. Kleinman is not a party to any lawsuit. Clearly, your perspective is different, and that's why we invite that. We try to be respectful to witnesses and to colleagues, so I appreciate that you feel passionately about this issue, but I think it's important to point out that you indeed have a professional, not legal conflict of interest, but a perspective that comes from your relationship with corporate chemical companies and oil companies, and I think that's important to put on the record." Dr. Williams agreed that her conclusion was fair.

Next Ortiz called on Erin Brockovich. Brockovich opened by telling the committee that she had learned about a potential cancer problem at the high school then researched via the Internet. "I was surprised to learn that the facility at the high school was producing 740 barrels of crude and processing over 300,000 cubic feet of natural gas per day. I had no idea that there was this type of production facility on a school campus." She quoted an Environmental Protection Agency newsletter that stated, "The oil industry has developed creative facades to mask its oil operations amid the glamour of Beverly Hills. For example, the Venoco Oil Company has built a 16-story tower on the Beverly Hills High School campus, painted in a floral design to hide a well."

After initiating a Freedom of Information request to all state agencies, she received documents that indicated there might be a problem at the school. One document in particular "disturbed" her and she quoted from the 1984 environmental checklist form completed by the oil company and requested by the city of Beverly Hills, who oversaw the operation. According to Erin, the environmental review board had asked the following questions:

> 1. Will the proposed oil platform result in substantial air emissions or deterioration of the ambient air? Their response was "maybe."
>
> 2. Does the proposed involve a risk of an explosion or the release of a hazardous substance? Their response was "maybe."
>
> 3. Will the proposed result in the creation of any health hazard or exposure of people to potential health hazards? Their response was "maybe."

The previous Environmental Impact Report (EIR), in 1978, addressed noise problems and aesthetics, not possible environmental or health effects. "They did mention the air but stated that no air monitoring could be done since emissions would be dispersed within a few thousand feet. We know in this report that there will be emissions, and I'm assuming that they saw the school sitting there and that children would be within and underneath those few thousand feet, but no one's going to bother to monitor the air. This EIR appears to be defective."

Erin was troubled that the city and school district would earn a 5 percent overriding royalty, potentially reaching $50 million. She voiced strong opposition to the city's earning money from an operation "that is dangerous to children." She continued, "The city . . . and the school district in charge of these children is earning money from an oil production facility that sits right on top, not adjacent to, a school that they know might explode, that might deteriorate the air, and might harm people. You can call me jaded. I think this is a serious conflict."

She was surprised no state agency had tested or monitored the air at the site despite the fact that in 1984 complaints were filed with the city stating serious concerns about the dangers of an explosion. "These citizens claim that the California Environmental Quality Act had been violated, and they wanted the operation shut down. These concerns went unheard. From 1984 until we came along in 2003, it appears no one did or said anything about this situation."

Erin told the committee about her testing and the resultant CBS story. "On February 6th, the South Coast Air Quality Management District sent inspectors to the site and, to their surprise, found that Venoco was venting natural gas into the air and that children were playing within 100 feet of this stack. On the night of February 6th, the AQMD did testing and confirmed that formation gas was being vented into the air and found benzene at the well vent at 4.5 ppm [parts per million] and found N-hexane at 12 ppm. These are the same compounds we found."

Defending her own testing and results, she accused Venoco of "operating its usual way—unattended—and thought no one was watching," noting that every time "Venoco or AQMD did tests, they made sure that prior to that, all leaks were fixed and sealed and then took their air test."

Erin listed the recent historical aspects of the case, saying, "On February 7th, AQMD inspectors sent a memo to the executive director, noting that the inspector's greatest concern was the children and that any parent should be concerned about their child in this type of environment.

"On February 11th, the AQMD assures us all is well; yet, on that very night, inspectors found significant levels of fugitive emissions coming from the facility and wrote an email to the executive officer stating that they were concerned for the inspectors' safety due to a potential explosion factor.

"In another email to the executive officer, the field inspector states: 'I cannot stress enough that this is becoming an immediate health and safety issue; not because of chronic effects, but due to the possibility of an explosion.' He goes on to note that the electrical system is suspect and that there is no vapor recovery to speak of. 'High levels of methane gas are emanating from this operation, and they have a faulty electrical system.' The inspector, in all of his experience, is convinced that each hatch is leaking in excess of 100,000 ppm of volatile compounds."

She went on to cite violations and chemical leaks in February, March, and throughout April. "There were serious leaking emissions from the operation, and the clarifier pit had extremely high levels of benzene and toluene that were volatilizing into the atmosphere. The benzene readings were 480,000 parts per billion and the toluene readings were 1,200,000 parts per billion.

"Shortly hereafter, the AQMD confirms through their own data that this non-permitted amine unit, even though Venoco had applied for it four years earlier, did in fact have a toxic cancer risk of 31 in a million."

Erin informed the panel that the Los Angeles District Attorney's Office, despite the obvious violations, was not able to proceed with any criminal actions due to Health and Safety

Code 42400.7, which states paying a civil fine precludes companies from criminal prosecution.

Citing methane concerns, she quoted the Camp Dresser and McKee findings of methane gas on the school campus at 227,000 ppm. "This is well above explosive limits. I'm curious why the Department of Toxic Substances Control has the authority and discretion to deed-restrict land for future school use that has methane gas in excess of 50,000 ppm, yet they have no authority over an existing school that is clearly in danger."

In summarizing her position, she stated, "This isn't about whether we found benzene in the air on a given day and the AQMD didn't. This is about a situation at a public school that has an oil and gas operation on its campus and is dangerous to the children. The AQMD has confirmed that there is a toxic cancer risk at this school. AQMD Rules 1401 and 1402 state that if you exceed a toxic cancer risk of 10 and/or 25 in a million they must give public notice. The AQMD has confirmed that this facility is leaking fugitive emissions at an alarming rate into the air. AQMD has confirmed high levels of benzene and toluene in the open pits that are volatilizing into the air."

Stating her belief the operation is unsafe, she asked the committee to consider:

1. Revisiting, rewriting, or rescinding Health and Safety Code Section 42400.7. I believe that health and safety codes need to protect the public.

2. Due to a serious conflict of interest, we ask that the city of Beverly Hills voluntarily remove themselves as lead agency and allow the Department of Toxic Substances Control to oversee the school and do a thorough risk assessment. If a voluntary action does not occur, we request that the state direct it to do so.

3. DTSC needs to have authority over all schools, existing

as well as future. Venoco has been allowed way too long to self-monitor. We need the appropriate state agency to oversee any industry on or adjacent to a public school.

4. We are very concerned that agencies have not been forthcoming with information. Public records are being denied and withheld. Information is being redacted. If necessary, we ask that a state legislative subpoena be sent to the city, the school district, and AQMD so that all records and information can be provided to the public.

And last, we absolutely believe that Venoco has no business operating this type of facility on a school campus or, frankly, anywhere else in the State of California.

Brockovich's two experts, both hired by the plaintiffs as part of the litigation, were each given twenty minutes. During that time they largely reiterated Erin's facts and figures and historical perspective of recent events pertaining to the wells. However, during part of their testimony they touched on Sempra and its permit.

Matt Hagemann, a former senior science policy advisor for the EPA, explained, "AQMD also has authority under the Clean Air Act for Title V—a program for major sources of air contaminants. The Sempra facility is in the queue for a permit. It has not gotten its permit, to date, despite the fact that in 1997 it was one of the top emitters of nitrous oxide in the South Coast Air Basin. Venoco, itself, has been considered for Title V, but further consideration is apparently not at hand.

"The Air Quality Management District also has authority for what is known as AB 2588, the Toxic Hot Spots Act. This requires facilities to report their air toxins and to ascertain the health risks from those air toxins. To date, AQMD has not required this type of risk assessment for Venoco or Sempra, and they have, actually, the discretion to require this sort of assessment for facilities combined when they are in close proximity. I believe that that should be considered. Venoco alone exceeds the AQMD priority threshold of 10 in a million risk under this rule."

Senator Aanestad addressed Erin. "Ms. Brockovich, on your recommendations that you would like to see this panel do, you made the statement that the agencies have not been forthcoming, and you would like to see this legislature use subpoena power to get the data.

"Let me just read you a list of studies and reports that I read before coming down to this meeting: California Department of Toxics; USC Cancer Registry; AQMD; Beverly Hills Fire Department; Camp Dresser & McKee report; California Department of Health Services; California Conservation Division of Oil, Gas & Geothermal Resources; South Coast Air Quality Management District; —— Group Study; Los Angeles County Environmental.

"I got those reports. I read them. What more reports are you talking about where people have not been forthcoming? Because I don't think there are any other reports. The only report I couldn't find was yours and what you based your lawsuit on. In fact, I understand the city of Beverly Hills had to subpoena your firm to get those reports and that there weren't, really, any."

Erin answered by saying she was not addressing the litigation today, only public policy. Then she continued that she was concerned when parents like Jody Kleinman, "who have called the AQMD, done a Public Records Act request, and they do not believe that they have gotten the appropriate information; and/or a reporter who gets information on public records and it's a blank page or it's stamped 'redacted.'"

Aanestad suggested parents contact their senator's office or his office and he would supply them with the information, "maybe not to their satisfaction but certainly to mine.

"Ms. Brockovich, you made statements in the press that I have seen, that the cancer rate of Beverly Hills alumni is 20 to 30 times that of the national average. Can you cite any epidemiological study or any credible scientific effort to support that kind of a claim?"

She called the claims "preliminary information" for the litigation then admitted, "But no, I think an epidemiological study or any information that you're willing to tell us is important, and our concern, again, is the fact that this is a facility that has existed since 1981; that hasn't had the appropriate testing done, that has current information that it is dangerous, and we don't think it has any business being on top of children." The senator pushed her for an answer, to which she responded, "In the beginning of this, we were working with a toxicologist who had made some preliminary findings, and I made reference to those."

He continued to pin Erin down on the facts despite her insistence she could not answer because of the pending litigation. Aanestad went on as the proceedings took a combative turn. "We had two parents here both testifying, both with children in the school, who have not taken their kids out of the school district; who said that, yes, there may be a risk—they don't know—but certainly, nothing is cause enough for a parent to take their children out of harm's way. Yet, you say that the Beverly Hills High School environment is dangerous to children. And I'm assuming that's because you think that there are health-related problems to the environment at that school. Can you give us any scientific, or any data that you might have? Because I can tell you, these nine different agencies, ten different agencies that I wrote, all came up with a negative report. A negative report. So, there must be something that you have, either in your law firm or in your possession, that says that, yes, there is a danger to these children—when all of these agencies and these two parents are saying, no, there isn't."

Brockovich shot back that she thought he had a problem with an agency.

"Ten of them?" Aanestad asked.

"And I think it could be, potentially, AQMD," she responded.

"Two parents. Maybe we have a problem with the legal system."

Ortiz was not happy with Aanestad's blatant accusations about Erin's intentions or his swipe at tort law and immediately came to her defense. Then, because the speakers had gone over time, she concluded the "Community Concerns About Beverly Hills High School" panel and went on to alter the agenda and asked the regulatory agency speakers to come forward. She had not allowed the city to respond to the allegations before closing the Beverly Hills part of the panel but promised Larry Weiner, the city's attorney, that he would be allowed to speak after the agencies.

When Dr. Barry Wallerstein, executive officer with the South Coast Air Quality Management District, was given his turn to speak, he explained his credentials and noted, "Just so the committee is aware, I'm a 1971 graduate of Beverly Hills High School; so I have familiarity with the campus."

He showed slides and then said, "I wanted to point out that we have nearly 27,000 facilities under permit, holding 60,000 permits, and tens of thousands of other facilities that fall subject to our regulation. We have a twelve-member governing board. Senator Alarcón was previously a member of our board.

"Relative to this issue, our mission is, quite simply, to protect public health from air pollution. Our interest in this issue has been to protect the kids, the teachers, the community members, and, at the same time, to be mindful that we need to be sensitive to treating fairly the operator. We have world-recognized expertise in monitoring, source testing, rule-development, permits, and enforcement. In fact, our rules are most frequently considered the most stringent anywhere in the nation."

Wallerstein spoke about his staff and their credentials, including scientists and engineers with advanced degrees. He highlighted their active enforcement program and that they had assessed the largest penalty of any local air district for an air quality violation anywhere in the country, "so, we're not soft on businesses."

Senator Escutia interrupted to notify members that Wallerstein's testimony would not include consultations between the AQMD and the district attorney concerning Venoco's violations since it related to an active criminal investigation. Wallerstein surprised the senator by announcing that his chief prosecutor was in attendance. Peter Mieras, chief prosecutor at the AQMD, then informed the committee that there was no active criminal investigation. Stanley Williams, from the Los Angeles County District Attorney's Office, interrupted Mieras. He contradicted Mieras and announced that there was, in fact, a pending investigation, and it was concluded that Wallerstein could not answer questions about that investigation.

Wallerstein, reclaiming the floor, explained to the panel that "while we have some expertise, we do not consider ourselves the ultimate experts in epidemiological issues, radiation exposure, hazardous soil analysis, water quality, or explosion risks in terms of the probability of explosion, although our staff are trained to be able to detect explosion risk."

Then he verbalized his account of the events, beginning with the airing of the CBS story. "We were contacted by the local CBS affiliate. They said they had some air samples from Southern California; would we come on camera and comment about the high levels of pollutants in those samples. They initially didn't tell us where the samples were taken. Over about a two-week period, we came to learn they were taken in Beverly Hills and ultimately at Beverly Hills High School. We had an opportunity to talk to the lab that analyzed the samples, and it was, in our judgment, that we should in fact just go out and sample ourselves after having that discussion, and then we would be prepared to talk about what the pollution levels might be on the campus.

"Before we went to the campus, we contacted the school district to let them know we were going to sample on their campus. At that point, we became aware of the litigation— or pending litigation at that point—that was involved in this matter. Again, we've just gone about doing our work and tried to stay out of the litigation."

He pointed out the amount of time they had spent on the situation at Beverly, noting they had visited the facility 31 times in 2003. "That is not normal when you have 27,000 facilities. We've received two odor complaints, although we were not able to confirm those. But what I would like to point out is we looked at past records, and in recent years we haven't had any public nuisance complaints like odors, and that's the sort of thing that would draw an oil well facility to our immediate attention. That was not occurring in this case."

Dr. Wallerstein displayed the sampling device used by all testing participants. "There's been a lot said about the sampling devices and how we sampled. I want to assure the committee that we have sampled properly. There are some limitations to how you interpret the data, but the samples were taken and analyzed properly. This is what the Masry law firm used. This is what we've used. This is what the city of Beverly Hills' consultant's using. It's a canister. It's clean, so it doesn't have any pollutants on the inside. It's put under a vacuum. We have a valve up here that slowly sucks the air in, in the case of most of our samples, over an eight-hour period. Then we bring the canister back to the laboratory, and we analyze the sample. Because of the sensitivity of this matter, I also want the committee to know that when we went out to sample, I had staff members watch these canisters for the full eight hours. They did not leave the canisters. So, we believe that we've gone through all the proper steps to prepare the canisters and then to collect the samples, chain of custody, and to analyze the samples."

He then pointedly noted that Hagemann, Brockovich's own expert, said in his earlier testimony that an agency needed to be doing the sampling for the sample to be valid. Wallerstein showed slides of the testing locations and the sampling, concluding, "we sampled in the bleachers of the athletic field, on the softball field. . . . We sampled on the Venoco property itself, adjacent to the equipment, and adjacent to the large boulevard (Olympic Boulevard) because we suspected we would get our highest pollutant concentrations there. Because of my familiarity with the area, I also wanted to sample at the park, which is catty-corner to the campus—Roxbury Park. It's used by many youth, athletic teams, as well as seniors who go bowling there—lawn bowling. And I wanted us to be comprehensive about the issue."

He showed other slides to verify samples on various dates. Then he addressed claims they sampled when the facility wasn't operating, when they were producing only gas, and when they were in full production of oil and gas. "I think we've covered a whole gambit of potential operating conditions, and we've been doing it at multiple locations. And the integrated means that we were doing—in essence, eight-hour samples—the grab samples are instantaneous samples."

He also pointed out the source samples, saying they had taken a number of samples at the well, directly from their pipes, before gases were emitted and diffused in the air. "So, some of the concentrations of benzene that have been reported in the press are in the pipe. It's not what someone breathes."

Senator Kuehl interrupted him to explain his statement concerning cancer risks at the site, which Wallerstein said were "below which no adverse non-cancer health effects are anticipated." She asked, "Is there a different measurement for cancer-related health effects?"

When Wallerstein answered that typically, the non-cancer health effects are at a lower level than the cancer health effects, she probed further. "So, if you're saying a lower level, do you mean that you'd find it with fewer particles? There would be a cancer risk?"

Wallerstein explained that it is above these levels that a health concern exists and introduced Dr. Jean Ospital, health effects expert. Dr. Ospital described, "Reference exposure limits are set for non-cancer effects because these effects are thought to have a threshold below which no effects occur. So, you'd have to be above that toxic threshold to get the effect. And what OEHHA [Office of Environmental Health Hazard Assessment] does is apply various safety factors to data—either from occupational studies or laboratory studies that show levels of health effects—apply these safety factors and come up with what they call the 'reference exposure level.'" She went on to explain that for cancer effects for most substances, it's assumed that there is no threshold.

"The way cancer-causing chemicals work is they can interact with our genetic material. So, theoretically, very few molecules can cause damage and result in a cell changing its metabolism and turning into a cancer cell. So, the way they do that is to come up with a risk or probability of cancer based on the exposure. So, there's a continuing gradient. The higher the exposure, of course, the higher the risk, and there is no threshold."

Dr. Ospital continued, "The way cancer risks are derived, cancer is a disease that takes many years to develop. That's what's called a long latency period. So, you may have ten, twenty, forty years' worth of exposure before you get cancer." Using cigarette smoking as a classic example, she said most of the cancer increases in cigarette smokers do not occur until after fifty. "There would be a gradient based on the exposure, and those exposures are assumed to occur over a lifetime—seventy or a lifetime."

When everyone was satisfied with the explanation, Wallerstein returned to his slide presentation, pointing out sampling data from the Venoco site in addition to sampling sites in the bleachers and the ball field. He then compared it to the Masry data from the KCBS report. What was ultimately revealed in Wallerstein's charts was a higher level of acetone and toluene, displayed publically for the first time. Acetone was measured at 56 and 41 parts per billion at the Venoco site, while the high toluene levels, at about 17 parts per billion, were found at the school's bleachers. Even with those unexpectedly high number, the AQMD was "unable to match what the Masry law firm found; and what we found . . . does correlate, with the exception of the toluene measurement, fairly well with ambient air in Southern California." Wallerstein also compared the AQMD data to the data from the city of Beverly Hills' sampling, and these correllated as well, including some significantly higher levels of acetone.

He explained that the reading of toluene, while higher than expected, was not high enough to label as an acute problem. He added that the school's maintenance shop is about 300 feet upwind of the bleachers where they sampled, so he was uncertain if maintenance work was a potential source. Since toluene material is typically found in paints and solvents, "We had revisited the high school, talked to the maintenance people, visited the Venoco facility, to see if we could discover where the toluene might be coming from, and at this point we don't have a conclusive answer."

Senator Alarcón asked about the federal standard for acetone. Wallerstein answered, "The reason that we haven't shown an REL [reference exposure level] for acetone is because there isn't one. Right now it's not listed as an air toxic. The acetone levels in the Masry samples were also very high for what you would expect to find in typical air, but it's, again, indicative traditionally of paint and solvent use, not of oil well operations."

Summarizing, he said, "Direct monitoring through the canister samples is one high sample of toluene (February of this year); otherwise, everything else looks to be within normal ranges. Some of the light hydrocarbons, the other hydrocarbons, are below levels that we would consider harmful, at least in our samples. And we were not able to duplicate the data of the Masry law firm."

Wallerstein then continued with a discussion of risk assessments. "There's two techniques that are generally used. One is to go out and take ambient samples. Generally, that's done for at least a year so you can cover all the seasons and weather conditions and changes in the wind, and then you can use that data through the risk assessment techniques and models.

"The other approach is to use emission factors and source tests from the facility itself and then run that through a model. Obviously, when we take a canister sample, that's what's in the air at the moment that sample's taken. It's nothing more, nothing less.

After illustrating that the air in Beverly Hills shows no abnormality compared to air elsewhere in the region, he showed a slide explaining that 70 percent of the carcinogenic risk in the air in California is driven by diesel emissions. "The other major drivers are 1, 3 butadiene from combustion processes and benzene from combustion processes, and the fueling of gasoline-powered vehicles. The data—this is out of our main study—for Beverly Hills as a community is about a thousand in a million."

Responding to comments about Notices of Violation at the Venoco site, he explained that the penalties the AQMD imposed upon the oil company were strict. He said the settlement for the violations had a total value at the time of over $70,000. In addition to fees, "We restricted their permit very clearly: no further venting of gas. They had to put a rupture disk in the vent that would set off an alarm if they ever vent again. In addition to that, we have required fence-line monitoring along the two fences that border the high school campus, which is an open-path, infrared, hydrocarbon analyzer that will set off an alarm. We'll be notified. There's a provision in the agreement for Venoco to work out a way of notification with the high school as well." Wallerstein explained they had included fence-line monitoring in the agreement instead of taking cash, to help address community concerns.

Mr. Mieras, the chief prosecutor for AQMD, next led a discussion of the penalties against Venoco. Regarding the first of three Notices of Violation, he explained that Venoco had not been cited for operating without a permit, as had been erroneously listed in one notice, because they had an application on file that allowed them temporary authority to operate. Instead of penalizing the company for that assessment, the Notice of Violation "covered the days that the produced gas was vented through the stack because they were no longer able to sell gas to the gas company. . . . That did not exceed thirty days. . . . So, there's thirty days associated for the first Notice of Violation.

"The second Notice of Violation, Venoco was cited for having fugitive leaks on four [*sic*] days: April 6th, April 10th, and April 19th. So, there's three more days. That makes it 33 days total.

"The third Notice of Violation, Venoco was cited for hooking up some carbon absorbers for the amine unit, which is a violation of our Rule 201. That's a one-day violation."

As there was no evidence that Venoco "intentionally, deliberately, willfully created these violations," they were assessed a penalty of $10,000 a day, with a maximum total fine of $350,000. "Now, under Section 42403 of the Health and Safety Code, there's a legislative mandate that we consider eight mitigation factors in assessing the penalties. . . . You have to arrive at an adjusted penalty applying these mitigation factors. These factors include such things as past compliance history and the response to the violation by the operator. Venoco had no compliance history with the district, so they were a first-time violator with respect to each of these types of violations. They also were very, very cooperative and responsive when we contacted them about these problems. They immediately stopped venting gas when we asked them to, and they stayed shut in for, I think, up to six months throughout this entire process. They produced their books and records as requested. They were cooperative on the inspections. And as Dr. Wallerstein indicated, we inspected them some 31 times in the past year. And there are other factors listed in 42403, all of which must be considered.

"So, in my judgment, mitigating the $350,000 maximum potential penalty to a figure of $70,000 was reasonable under the circumstances, and that's the penalty that we assessed. I'm learning for the first time today that, actually, the monitoring may amount to a total of $100,000."

Dr. Wallerstein then assured the panel that the AQMD staff frequently returned to the site to ensure the facility's compliance with the rules and regulations and that repairs have been made. They were also requiring Venoco to conduct a full risk assessment, using emission factors and source samples, due no later than the end of that month. As a result of the events surrounding the Venoco site, AQMD decided that because they had not been placing a high priority on oil wells, they would use field staff to inspect 185 additional facilities, and part of that inspection was to target facilities in close proximity to schools. "In addition to that, we have adopted a regulation to tighten up emission control requirements for oil well operations within our jurisdiction. We believe that this newly adopted regulation adopted last week is as tight or tighter than any provision elsewhere in the state, and we have incorporated stricter requirements for facilities that are within 500 feet—or, excuse me, 333 feet of a school."

Wallerstein next addressed hexane. "In the early press

reports, there was a researcher using the Masry data that said the hexane concentration of 38 parts per million was of concern to him. We think when you actually look at the laboratory report, it wasn't reported just as hexane. It included hexane and all other carbon molecules heavier than a C6. There are other molecules mixed into there, so it's not a 38 part per million reading of hexane in that sample.

"The next issue you've heard about today is explosion, and I want to emphasize that we direct our staff to take a precautionary approach. So, when we discovered the first time we went out there they were venting gas, they were doing it at 165 feet in the air. But from our perspective, there's a school campus and there's a hospital behind it. We looked at their permit. We told them to stop and desist. We've since done some modeling that would not have created an explosion risk at ground level because it dilutes in the air from 165 feet as it moves out towards the ground." He then went on to discuss the explosive limit and measurements, using figures to illustrate why they didn't believe there was a potential problem at the site.

Sempra Energy was also mentioned and Wallerstein said it was not a very large pollution source, such as a large power plant, and although it is under federal law classed as a substantial pollution source, it is within what is considered safe limits.

After presenting risk assessments, he presented the AQMD's intent to continue oversight by implementation of the fence-line monitoring, periodic sampling with canisters, and inspection of the facility. He recommended better agency coordination and suggested that the California EPA could develop with other authorities a screening procedure where when "something rises to a level, then we all go to work.

But, obviously, as you've listened to me talk about this and heard from others, there's a balancing act here between the amount of resources you pour into something and the basis upon which you're pouring those resources that are vitally needed in other areas in terms of health risk."

After offering additional suggestions, Wallerstein said, "We think we've discharged our legal duty. We're not perfect, but we've really applied a lot of resources and tried to properly address this issue, and we're not finished. Lastly, there were some comments about getting public records from us. If someone has a problem with that, all they have to do is contact me. If they didn't receive some things, it may be because they're protected under law as confidential materials so that a facility isn't at an economic disadvantage while one of its competitors seeks certain information. We don't have anything to hide. We're available to talk to people when they would like to talk to us about this matter and our activities."

In response to Kuehl's questions about safety at the site, Wallerstein said, "The hardest question I've had in these many months in listening to parents—because I've talked to many parents, crying parents, pulling their kids from the school or athletic teams—is should they have their child at this school? I told them they had to answer that for themselves, but I also told them, just based on this information—it could change with new information—but based on the information we have at hand, I would allow my child to attend that school."

After allowing representatives from the district attorney's office as well as the oil and gas industry to share their testimony, Senator Escutia called Beverly Hills city attorney Larry Wiener to speak, although some of the committee members were no longer present, including Senator Ortiz, who had initiated the panel. Wiener's testimony at times duplicated information previously provided, but he opened with a personal comment. "It's interesting—we started the hearing this afternoon with testimony from parents, and we are really ending the hearing with testimony from parents. As Vice Mayor Egerman indicated, he was a graduate, as was his wife, of the high school. His children went to the high school. The mayor's daughter is currently a senior at the high school. Other councilmembers have graduated from the high school. I am a graduate of the high school. The superintendent's son is a sophomore at the high school. The board members' children are all at the high school or at the junior high level and will be at the high school.

"When we heard about this issue, the first night of sweeps week on CBS, we were shocked first of all, and we were immediately concerned if there might be a problem at Beverly Hills High School. And we didn't assume there was or there wasn't. We knew that once this issue had been raised, that it was going to be our job as the governing boards of those two agencies to do our due diligence and ensure the community that there had been adequate testing done at the high school; that these allegations were investigated and that there was an answer one way or another."

Wiener applauded the AQMD for their prompt response. "The AQMD was at the site immediately, as their slide indicated earlier, and testing throughout the spring and providing memos to the community—which were posted on the school district's website for the community to read— throughout the spring as testing was done. And I think that brought some measure of interim relief to the community because there was a great deal of consternation when these allegations first surfaced."

He told about the city's determination to allay any fears

the site was unsafe. "What the city and the school district decided to do working together was to first search for an environmental testing firm that could provide us with the information that we needed. We found an outfit— Camp Dresser & McKee (CDM), which is a national firm, nationally recognized; works in Southern California with school districts; works under the supervision of the DTSC on various school sites—and we told them that we needed an investigation that's going to give us the information we need as parents and tell us whether or not that school site is safe and we can continue to send our students there or whether we need to do something to make it safe."

CDM informed the city of the necessary guidelines for successful testing, telling them, "'We need three things from you. We need to do air sampling; we need to do soil sampling; and we need to do soil gas sampling.' We basically, at that point, as Vice Mayor Egerman said, wrote them a blank check. We said, 'Okay, you design the testing protocols to tell us what we need to know, and by the way, we need to know that before school starts in the fall because we are not going to send students back to that school site unless we have the report that tells us either that it's safe or that it's not safe and here's what you need to do to make it safe or to keep the kids off those fields.'"

He confirmed that by August, more than two hundred samples of air and soil and soil gas had been taken and all findings were consistent with the AQMD testing. "We tested in December of 2003, and again the report came back consistent with the previous tests. And we will be testing again in 2004 periodically to make sure that the results stay consistent. . . .

"There is not one piece of data, not one report, that we have not made public and that is not available either by going to the website to see the executive summaries . . . or by coming to our office and asking for all of the technical backup."

The city had also initiated local legislative proceedings. "We had requested information from the Masry & Vititoe firm. We had requested that they provide us with any testing data they had and any epidemiological data that they had which would have supported the claims of excess numbers of cancers. We were not provided that information. At one time we received a letter that said, 'If you provide us your data, we'll provide you our data.' We sent our data, but we still never received the data from that law firm."

Wiener discussed the subpoenas and the failure to comply, relating how the city requested testing information from not only the Masry & Vititoe firm but also Baron and Budd, "the Texas law firm that is actually taking the lead on litigating the lawsuit that we're not talking about today." He described, "We had to go to court to enforce those subpoenas, and eventually, under a threat of contempt of court from Judge Baker of Los Angeles County Superior Court, we did receive the data. Well, we received some testing data. We received no epidemiological data because what was told to us in court is that no epidemiological study had been conducted. And so, that was again reaffirmed in a letter just last week: that there was no epidemiological study conducted that would show that there's an excess number of cancers among Beverly Hills alumni."

Wiener informed the panel that the information they had received—eight days of test results—indicated background levels of nondetect or one part per million for benzene, the chemical of most concern. Two of the eight days of testing showed elevated levels of benzene, but on the first day, a Sunday in November 2002, the benzene spike measured half of the chronic reference exposure limit. "That day, there was a spike of benzene, but none of the spike of toluene or ethyl benzene or xylene that one would expect if you were actually seeing emissions from an oil well. CDM said there is a spike of benzene there in the data, but that wouldn't have been coming from oil emissions because you would have seen a concurrent spike in toluene and ethyl benzene and xylene and other chemicals associated with oil and natural gas.

"They suggested more testing based on those results and as we looked at the data, we saw Masry & Vititoe had gone out and done more testing in December and saw nothing unusual in the December tests, the Saturday and Sunday in December." Then, in January, the firm had two samples taken at the high school, an eight-hour canister sample and a grab sample. "The eight-hour sample showed, again, a nondetect or background level for benzene—the principal chemical of concern, as we understand it. The grab sample showed the highest reading that was received, which was the 17 parts per billion, which is, again, above background, just slightly under the chronic reference exposure limit.

"Again, we asked CDM, 'What do you make of this?' CDM told us that it is highly anomalous that you would have co-located samples—two samples located in the same place— one showing nondetect; one showing such a high reading compared to background." They suggested more testing.

"And frankly, that's what we did. We had been doing that additional testing all throughout 2003. So, after reviewing all of the data, we believe that the testing as a whole shows us that the conditions at the high school are not unusual. And frankly, nothing that I have heard here today has convinced me otherwise. In fact, during some of the events discussed in the emails and the AQMD violations, at the same time the AQMD was taking readings of the ambient air on the campus and showing no impact to the campus air from what was going on at the oil well site."

Wiener stated the city was fairly confident that they had seen the worst-case conditions, during which they were sampling air without any impact on the campus. He referenced one independent agency's review of epidemiological data, the Cancer Surveillance Program at the University of Southern California's Keck School of Medicine. "That program took a look at data that involved residents in Beverly Hills, not BHHS alumni. They had found no cancers beyond what one would expect for this demographic.

"No elevated rates of cancer among those cancers that were being identified at the time in the media as being of concern—Hodgkin's lymphoma and non-Hodgkin's lymphoma and thyroid cancer—in the population of Beverly Hills. And I think we felt from the city perspective that, certainly, if there were a problem coming from that oil well, we would think that we would see it in the residential population as well as the alumni population. But that is the only scientific evaluation of epidemiological data that has been done."

He addressed the 1984 environmental checklist allegations made earlier by Brockovich. "A look at the list showed that it's not that there was nothing followed up on. 'Maybe' is checked. And at the back where it says 'All Responses' you refer to the 1978 EIR. It's not that it was ignored. . . . Now, it was referenced that this 1978 EIR spoke of nothing but noise and odors. . . . I can assure you that if you go through this document—and it's not a thin document—there is far more than noise and odors discussed. . . .

"We will continue to do that monitoring, and we will continue to do that research, and we will continue to rely on the AQMD and any other agency that wishes to do research."

In response to Kuehl's question about Department of Toxic Substance Control's involvement, Wiener responded, "When this first became public, when we first learned about this through the news media, it was all about air emissions. The AQMD immediately was out at the site, and we were working with the AQMD. And I believe that there was a letter early on from the DTSC offering their services if we cared to use them. At that time, we were working with the AQMD, and I don't think we took advantage of that. We didn't follow up on it.

"A couple of months later . . . we did engage in discussions with the DTSC at that time about having them come onto the site and join us in this testing. We offered to split samples with them and have them review our data. Our data is available to them if they'd like to see it now.

"At that point . . . their process was three to six months. They were very forthcoming; and they promised at that point that they would do everything they could to meet our timetable. And by the way, our timetable was what we had committed to parents—I think I mentioned this earlier—that we would have that testing done before school started in the fall of 2003. . . . But we felt that our best chance of meeting that timetable was to not stop and switch horses and start with the DTSC program but instead to continue on the path that we had already begun to go down with CDM. . . . We finished about a week-and-a-half before school started."

Kuehl asked about ongoing monitoring at the site. "We found nothing abnormal in terms of toxic substances. We did find a pocket of methane . . . not at 5 feet, and it was not at surface level, but it was at 15 feet below ground surface in the upper field near some asphalt basketball courts. That was delineated with step-out testing. There was testing that found it, and then we stepped out until we didn't find it anymore. So, we knew what the source was. . . . And what was recommended with regard to the methane was that we install methane sensors in the bathrooms that are adjacent to that field, which has been done, and that we regularly monitor the basement areas of the building surrounding the field, or nearest to the field—there really aren't buildings all the way surrounding the field—which is being done. . . .

"We know that we are going to have to continue to do monitoring over time. This is not an issue that is going to simply go away."

Senator Escutia was curious about the oil revenue agreement between the city and oil company. "I'm glad you asked about that because there's been an implication that somehow we would be influenced by royalty payments or money.

"We have gotten in the last few years—which is probably when we've gotten the most money from the oil wells as a result of rising oil prices, et cetera—the city and the school district have received between two and three hundred thousand dollars a year. The city's annual budget is $258 million. Two hundred fifty thousand out of a $258 million budget—this is not a number that is a significant revenue source to the city of Beverly Hills. . . . We have spent far more on testing than we do achieve in revenues, and we will continue to spend a lot of money on testing. . . . The revenue from that oil well is not influencing the actions of the city or the school board in this matter."

Beverly Hills parent Mahshid Soleimani spoke next and questioned the accuracy and integrity of the AQMD's investigation. "Time after time you will find inconsistency in their lab results and reports. On February 6, 2003, AQMD paid a surprise visit to Venoco's oil wells facility on Beverly Hills High School campus. AQMD found that Venoco was venting their unwanted gas into the air illegally. Samples were taken from the well gas directly at the vent pipe, and they were collected from ambient air around the high school. An executive office memorandum dated February 11, 2003, signed by AQMD's executive officer, Dr. Barry Wallerstein, reports that it's likely elevated acetone level was found in the evening sample but not the well gas and continues to indicate that such chemical species is not generally associated with oil well operation.

"But the draft report of the windpipe gas says a different story. The regional draft report stated that acetone was detected at less than 500 ppb in the gas collected directly from the windpipe. If acetone is not associated with the oil and gas operation, how would you explain the detection of about 500 ppb of acetone in the gas samples taken directly from the windpipe? The results from the regional draft analysis were changed later on, and acetone's presence was changed to 'not detected' and I do have attachments. . . .

"Acetone is detected, yet once again, this time, in extremely high levels at 200 ppb in the ambient air samples taken on the third week of April. Inspectors from AQMD are sent to investigate. A report prepared on May 28, 2003, by AQMD's Inspector Jeanette Holtzman, indicates that Venoco claims that the facility has no acetone on the site to date, nor in the past. So, one, Venoco would be eliminated as the possible source, and the final conclusion on the source of the acetone would be made by Mr. Ben Shaw, the senior lab manager at AQMD, that (quote) 'a storage paint shed at the high school is the most likely source of the acetone.'

"My question to Dr. Wallerstein and Mr. Shaw would be: If Venoco has never used acetone on their site and if acetone is not part of the natural gas pumped from the ground, then how would you explain the presence of 3,200 ppb of acetone in the waste water sample taken from the reinjection tank by Inspector Holtzman on April 8 of 2003?

"Waste water is the water that comes up mixed with oil and natural gas and has no outside contact and certainly no connection to the paint shed at the high school grounds.

"On Friday, February 21, 2004 (three weeks ago), I had a telephone conversation with Mr. Shaw. He denied that any acetone was ever detected in AQMD's test results, and my request for a meeting with him to share my findings was denied. I was also told by him, 'Do not call the inspectors. They are instructed not to speak to you.'

"For the past three or four days . . . I have put, at least, forward five telephone calls to Dr. Wallerstein's office for something that I needed to actually prepare this report, and I haven't been able to get it. . . . That report was denied to me."

Thomas White, chairman of the Municipal League of Beverly Hills, next addressed his opinion on the "disparities or points of view between some of the information. One is that the school district and the city of Beverly Hills, being, both, defendants in the current lawsuit, face the possibility of being held liable for billions of dollars in damages. I'm sure anyone in that position believing that their best interests primarily— or at least in the first instance—is to protect taxpayers from that type of liability, they're going to be very reluctant to make admissions, publicly or privately, that would have an impact on the trier of fact and on the lawsuit."

Kuehl asked White about the contract between the schools and Venoco: "So, if they were to cease operations, would they be liable under the contract?"

White responded that that was a concern. "We have asked politely if that would be considered, and the response has been, 'Well, we might be in breach of contract.' If you ask the same elected officials whether or not they would prefer not to have oil operations on the campus, they would say, 'In theory, yes.' But now that we're receiving income from it—which I would tend to go along with the city attorney that that, in itself, is probably not a significant factor—but over a long period of time, it can be a material factor. A much greater factor in the minds of decision-makers and even in the minds of parents whose children are in the schools is, 'What will happen if it turns out they're right? Will we have a school district?'"

White then reminded the panel that removing children from school could be a prohibitive expense for many residents. "There is only one [public] high school in Beverly Hills. If you send your child to a private school, you could expect to pay $50,000 a year. Sixty percent of the residents in Beverly Hills are apartment renters. They don't have that kind of money even for one child, let alone two."

Parent and BHHS alumni Janet Morris testified next, noting that she was not a plaintiff in any lawsuit, and referred to regulations prohibiting the well. "I believe that in the California Code of Regulations, Section 14010(h), it says that a school cannot be situated on that site—on a site that has oil pipelines underneath the school. . . . I am one of the people who thinks that operating a producing oil well at Beverly Hills High School is a threat to the health and safety of the students and the staff at the high school.

"I want to say at the outset that but for the lawsuit—the personal injury lawsuit that was filed—I don't believe that we'd be sitting here discussing this. I think that the city of Beverly Hills optimistically would have shut this down. As you know, the $300,000 a year is not significant to the city of Beverly Hills nor to the school district. So, why would we keep an oil well operating if we think there's a threat of health or safety if that's all we get?"

She disagreed that neither Venoco's response in requesting a California Environmental Quality Act exemption to the EIR nor the problems with the amine unit had caused public controversy. "There were over one hundred letters sent to the AQMD specifically responding to the licensing of the amine unit and saying specifically that we don't think that Venoco should be operating, especially without an Environmental Impact Report.

"Although the plans now are that the site will be equipped with electronic monitoring devices to detect the release and presence of toxic substances, the oil company Venoco is the one who monitors the controls and must notify AQMD if anything is amiss. I think we all agree that the fox should not be guarding the henhouse."

Beverly Hills activist Ari Bussel attempted to bring a human perspective to the proceedings. He began, "Our family moved to Beverly Hills in 1982. I was then a junior at Beverly Hills High School. My brother, my sister, and I all graduated from Beverly. Among the three of us, we have advanced degrees from Stanford, Harvard, and UCLA. We have five different advanced degrees. My brother is a cancer survivor and my sister. Both my brother and my sister are part of the litigation. They went through the whole four years at Beverly. I only went there two years.

"I think that the main difference for anyone who is sitting here and looking in the back is where are the parents? Where are today's parents? Where are the children? The silence is overwhelming, because if we go back to any one of the first town hall meetings, during which we didn't have any city official present, but they did get reports of it—and there are videos—person after person stood up and said, 'I'm [so-and-so]. I'm twenty-eight. I've benzene in my blood. I'm [so-and-so]. I'm twenty-seven. I have this horrible autoimmune disease.' And it went on and on and on without stop.

"Now, there was a question asked time and again: Has there been any epidemiological study done? And the answer is 'no.' There was another question asked time and again: Do we have any scientific studies about the effects of close proximity of oil drilling and gas venting on people at the ages of late teenage? And the answer again was 'no.'" He questioned why an epidemiological study had not been commissioned by an impartial body such as the PTA or the alumni association. Without a study, he said, there would be no way of determining the severity of the situation relative to the oil well.

"It is very easy to dismiss claims, but we really don't know is there causality. And I think that the main point is—and Senator Aanestad asked—let's clear the air. Let's see what is the real objective. And I will paraphrase what my brother said: It should never happen again. It should not happen to any parent that will have to face him or herself in the mirror, that will have to face his or her daughter or son and say, 'Why did it happen?' We don't know the causality. We don't know that it's the oil drilling or the gas venting or Sempra or the close proximity to Olympic Boulevard, which is the major artery. We simply don't know, but we need to investigate, and the investigation must be impartial, impartial meaning independent."

He concluded, "In summary, I think that what we should do and I think what the committee is trying to do is to take a proactive approach because we don't know exactly what is going on. . . .

"And I think that there was a very interesting comment earlier by one of the experts saying that cancer has a long latency period. We need to remember, and unfortunately you don't have the tools here, but I'm sure that the video can be provided from one of the first town hall meetings so you can see we're not talking about people in their late thirties, like I am, in their forties, fifties, or sixties. We're talking about people in their late twenties, in their early thirties, beautiful people that suddenly have autoimmune disease, that have things which are too horrible even to mention.

". . . For instance, what my sister has is quite rare or it's not representative. When you hear that there is another person that has exactly the unexplainable symptoms that all the top doctors in Beverly Hills could not after numerous tests, could not figure out what they were, and then you have a third person with very similar symptoms again, we don't want that to happen again. We don't know what causes it, but we need to find out, and I'm sure that our elected officials are doing their best to come up with an answer."

Senator Escutia thanked Bussel and said, "Thank you for recognizing that it is the desire of this committee to establish a proactive approach. As you well know, it is not the role of this committee to establish causality. That is the role of the courts. But it is very much the role of the state legislature to perhaps provide an adjustment to the statutory framework if, in fact, that is needed. And I think that, perhaps, after we get all the information and we have further hearings, such a statutory adjustment might be needed in order to prevent this, first of all, from happening again; second of all, to secure better enforcement, both at the civil and criminal level; obviously to promote better communications with the public; and also to better coordinate among all the agencies that have, perhaps, different jurisdictions."

Following Bussel, Marrina W., mother of a Beverly Hills graduate, spoke about her concerns over potential harm from radioactivity at the site. She was followed by activists Ruth Sarnoff and Patricia McPherson from the Grassroots

Coalition. These comments are available in the complete transcript. After these women spoke, the meeting was adjourned. At the end of the day, nothing came of the hearings that could or would address the issues at the high school.

12

The Fog Clears

Rather than love, than money, than fame, give me truth.
— Henry David Thoreau

When the benzene-laden fog cleared, how was the case against Beverly Hills resolved, and who ultimately benefitted from any monies given or received? The first of three summary judgments that changed the direction of the case and brought it to a close for Beverly Hills and its school district was filed in Los Angeles Superior Court on November 20 and 21, 2006. It involved only twelve out of the more than one thousand plaintiffs. Each plaintiff alleged that his or her respective illness had been caused by exposure to the various chemicals such as benzene, hexavalent chromium, and PCBs emitted from the Venoco site or related furans from Sempra's nearby facility. Finding for the defendants, Los Angeles Superior Court presiding judge Wendell Mortimer ruled that plaintiffs' experts lacked reliable evidence to establish that exposures to any or all of the chemicals were a substantial factor in causing any of the diseases. Thus, the defendant's motions on all grounds were granted.

In a detailed finding on December 12, 2006, Judge Mortimer wrote the following:

> None of the plaintiffs' experts can name any authoritative textbooks, peer-reviewed articles or regulatory organizations or scientific bodies that say that benzene causes any of the diseases in this case. Their opinions on causation are without support and speculative. Further, as discussed above under the heading of specific causation, plaintiffs' exposure levels were hundreds to thousands of times lower than levels associated with any risk and are thus trivial. Defendant's motions for summary judgment shifted the burden to plaintiffs and plaintiffs have not met their burden of proof to show a triable issue of fact.

Based on expert testimony offered, Mortimer concluded emission levels were not at levels dangerous enough to cause harm. He relied on the existing preponderance of testing data to arrive at his decision.

That first summary judgment paved the way for the city and school district to file the second and third, thereby concluding their portion of the legal wrangling. On January 9, 2007, the school district and city brought a summary judgment on the grounds that the Beverly Hills school district, as a governmental entity, is immune from liability. Finding for the city and school district, Judge Mortimer wrote:

> Defendants cite "A Century of California Law" which consists of a list of a dozen cases since 1906 generally standing for the proposition that the trial judge may exclude expert opinions which lack foundation or are based upon conjecture or speculation. They further cite California Evidence Code sections 801 (b) and 803 for authority. This court adopts that body of law and exercises its prerogative to examine the foundation and basis for the experts' opinions. Particularly

instructive are the cases of *Stephen v. Ford Motor Company* (2005) 134 CA 4th 1363, a non-suit case where it was stated that the expert's testimony was properly excluded because there was no foundation for his opinions or conclusions (page 1365) and the Lockheed Litigation cases 2004 115 CA 4th 558 which say Evidence Code section 801, subdivision b states that the court must determine whether the matter that the expert relies on is of a type that an expert reasonably can rely on in forming an opinion upon a subject to which his testimony relates. We construe this to mean that the matter relied on must provide a reasonable basis for the particular opinion offered and that an expert opinion based on speculation or conjecture is inadmissible (page 564). Plaintiffs urge the court to rely on the case of *Robert v. Andy's Termite & Pest Control, Inc* 203 113 CA 4th 893 for the proposition that the court lacks discretion to exclude plaintiffs' experts' causation testimony. However that case, unlike our case, involved novel scientific methodologies and a discussion of Kelly and Daubert standards of exclusion. More importantly, that case also said that the court had deprived plaintiff of the right to present evidence without complying with procedural rules, "by way of a motion for summary judgment before trial . . ." which is not the case here. Plaintiffs have had every opportunity to present evidence in opposition to the summary judgment motions and in the two days of oral argument.

At the same time, the city filed a motion for summary judgment based upon governmental tort liability issues. Los Angeles Superior Court judge William F. Highburger agreed to hear the motion: "Even though this court previously ruled in favor of all defendants, including the city of Beverly Hills, in a motion for summary judgment based upon medical causation in the first twelve bifurcated plaintiffs' cases, this motion will be ruled upon separately because of the different issues involved and the potentially broader implications to all the over one thousand remaining plaintiffs' cases."

Although the ruling on the first summary judgment entitled the city to file a 1038 motion to collect court costs from plaintiffs, after a series of meetings, the city worked out a settlement with Baron and Budd. They met with Russell Budd—Fred Baron had passed away—and ironed out a deal that they would file for minimal court costs if plaintiffs agreed not to appeal the city and school board's summary judgments, freeing them from further litigation. According to former school board president Myra Lurie, the potential to retrieve a greater amount of court costs was overshadowed by the aggravation and constant distractions continuing the case would have meant.

In a letter to the plaintiffs, Baron and Budd informed them, "The city currently has pending before the court of appeal a petition for writ of mandate seeking to require the trial court to hear the city's proposed section 1038 motion which plaintiffs have opposed. The motion seeks to recover from plaintiffs and their counsel its defense costs, including reasonable attorneys' fees, expert witness fees and other costs incurred in defending against plaintiffs' claims in Moss. The district has also indicated its intent to file a similar section 1038 motion." The letter states that counsel "strongly disagrees" with the bases for the 1038 motion by the public entities which, in essence, contend that the claims brought against them were frivolous and brought in bad faith. The law firm cautioned, "As we have seen in prior rulings however, the court's judgment on these issues is not predictable. Moreover, these section 1038 motions have risks for you, our clients, which we want to eliminate."

The letter went on to explain,

Under the terms of the General Release, the public entities will agree not to file or further pursue their section 1038 motions in connection with the Moss litigation, and further agree not to file any actions for malicious prosecution against the plaintiffs and plaintiffs' counsel.

In exchange the plaintiffs will dismiss all pending claims against the public entities in the Moss litigation, while preserving all claims against all other defendants, including, most critically, the oil company defendants. In addition, payments will be made to the public entities in the amount of $22,500 each or a total of $45,000. If our pending appeals from the orders granting the oil company defendants' medical causation motions for summary judgment are granted and the trial court's orders granting the medical causation motions for summary judgment in favor of the oil company defendants are overturned on appeal. Payments will be made to the public entities in the amount of $225,000 each ($450,000 total) if our appeals from the orders granting the oil company defendants' medical causation motions for summary judgment are instead denied or we withdraw our appeals.

It was then recommended that each plaintiff sign the enclosed general release, under which they would not be financially liable.

An appeal of the original summary judgment from November 2006 against the oil companies and Sempra was filed in Los Angeles Appellate Court. The last hearing was December 2, 2009, but was rescheduled for December 21, 2010. Beverly Hills and its school district both received payment from Baron and Budd and closed the case. As yet there has been no ruling on that appeal.

The half million dollars paid to the city may be explained by the settlement between Frontier Oil and the plaintiffs. A client meeting was held on October 10 and 11, 2007, in Los

Angeles to discuss a proposed settlement with the defendant Frontier Oil, as well as a resolution of claims with Beverly Hills and its school district. The plaintiffs unable to attend received a letter from Baron and Budd. In the letter, the firm indicated they were in the last stages of negotiating an agreement with Frontier Oil. They saw the amount of the settlement—$10 million—as a "positive development in the larger litigation." They were hopeful this event would spur other defendants to engage in settlement talks as well.

Despite my attempts to discern a motive, to this day Frontier's agreement to settle remains a mystery. Due to the confidentiality of the negotiations and settlement agreement, it is impossible to know for certain why, after a judgment in Frontier's favor, they elected to give Baron and Budd $10 million. Some speculate it was predicated on business or insurance liability, despite the fact the first summary judgment had excused them from causation. One attorney I asked said it is not unusual for insurance companies to do a cost effective analysis of the benefits of moving forward.

Dispersion of that money is another mystery. Verification of any financial considerations to plaintiffs is impossible due to confidentiality clauses. An attorney at Baron and Budd explained their process for selecting clients to receive money from the Frontier Oil settlement. Examining the population during the years covered within the settlement sets a limited exposure parameter. A toxicologist and doctor then determine the relationship between a plaintiff's disease and its liability to benzene. The search covered the entire plaintiff population of almost one thousand, specific to the time Frontier Oil owned the wells. Approximately four hundred plaintiffs received an undisclosed amount of money. Whether or not the settlements varied, the attorney would not disclose. He went on to say that he did not believe Baron and Budd recovered all their costs after the settlement. According to the plaintiffs' contingency fee agreement, Masry & Vititoe received 40 percent of the gross recovery, whether through settlement or judgment. If no money was recovered the attorneys received nothing. As co-counsel, Baron and Budd shared monies received as a result of the lawsuit on a "substantially equal basis."

Although millions were spent by the city and school districts, the insurance companies paid the bulk, with the city incurring costs the insurer denied.

The city's scare not only affected its pocketbook, it impacted the city's environmental policies. When he became mayor, Barry Brucker enacted a green program. The council passed legislation tightening restrictions and prohibiting expanded drilling at local drilling sites. "What the operator can do (which I do not think goes far enough) is that they can drill a new hole but must remove an old drill at the same time. So there can be no additional holes without eliminating an equal amount of drilling holes," Brucker described. Slant drilling from into Beverly Hills from outside city limits must conform to the same standards as within the city.

Brucker also says he will deny any new drilling requests from contracted oil companies. "If I had my way there would be a prohibition on any new drilling, period. The law, however, prohibits us from breaking the terms of the current contracts with vendors. We are forced to live with the decisions of our predecessors."

Brucker believes the city is more diligent today about monitoring the wells: "So far the perimeter monitoring sensors seem to be performing well and the scrutiny placed on the vendor is much more severe and conditional on accountability."

Sam Atwood of the AQMD said the methane monitors at the well are still operational as are the perimeter VOC monitoring sensors. "We have not received any complaints related to the Venoco facility since 2006." Atwood adds the last inspection was on April 30, 2009, [and AQMD inspectors found the facility in compliance with regulations]. "They found no leaks from the wastewater sump, vapor recovery unit, scrubbers, carbon canisters or the amine unit. Inspectors did, however, notice oil leaks at two tanks. As a result the operator instituted a more robust self-inspection routine for these tanks. A fence-line monitor is still operating to monitor VOC leaks and the methane monitor is functioning as well."

Beverly Hills fireman and inspector Chris Heyer says that although they are only required to inspect the facility once a year, they opt to visit every six months. "We are proactive about our oversight that covers a wide range of issues, including fire protection systems, egress, storage issues, fire- and sound-proofing material and numerous other maintenance-related and new technological improvements." Heyer says the state and the fire marshal also make regular visits.

He continues, "Department of Oil, Gas, and Geothermal Resources requires records be kept and submitted monthly. The site is surprisingly very well kept and maintained and they appear to be adamant about good housekeeping and testing. If there are any minor repairs they get back to us and before you know it we receive notice everything was done. I am really impressed by how quickly they react."

The City of Beverly Hills Building and Safety Department director George Chavez and his staff conduct unscheduled inspections at the site yearly and file a report and an update. One staff member said this element of surprise ensures they are getting a true picture of conditions.

The lease on the Venoco site will be revisited by the Beverly Hills Board of Education in 2016. There is no way to forecast who will sit on the board and what will be the extent of their institutional memory on the issue. Brucker, however, believes the lease will not be renewed. "We were locked into certain agreements and contracts previously negotiated and although we might have liked to change or alter these agreements, it wasn't possible." When asked whether the city, if allowed to do it again, would allow an oil well next to a school, Brucker responded empathically, "Never."

Rumors and rumblings of negotiations for a new lease are an undercurrent that has garnered the attention of the few remaining warriors on the scene. Since there is no institutional memory on the current school board save Myra Lurie, it is anybody's guess what the board's reaction may be. At the August 31, 2010, council meeting Jody Kleinman, Janet Morris, and Mashid Soleimani spoke up against renewing the well's lease and favored exercising any options at the city's disposal to effectively prevent such an occurrence.

Unlike the school board, there is a great deal of firsthand experience on the city council, including Barry Brucker, Jimmy Delshad, Dr. William Brien, and Nancy Krasne. To fend off resigning the lease, Brucker has asked City Attorney Larry Wiener to bring forward an amendment to the current Beverly Hills Municipal Code banning oil drilling within the city at the September council meeting.

Will they vote for it? Many factors will enter into the discussion. Money, experience with the issue, and, of course, politics.

13

A Community Lesson in Prevention

Democracy is the only system capable of reflecting the humanist premise of equilibrium or balance. The key to its secret is the involvement of the citizen.

—John Ralston Saul

The months-long discussion of cancer clusters and excess toxicity levels had made the community incredibly jumpy. Concern for the children at the school, fear for those who had attended previously, and sadness for those who were suffering with a disease permeated the fabric of the city. The mistrust and suspicion were legitimate and understandable, yet no concrete proof could be found to dispute the city's test results or validate the possible adverse health effects.

The Internet afforded amazing access to studies, and I spent many evenings after work and free moments searching for information that might shed a different light on the status quo. While I was attempting to learn about science and its practices, a red flag appeared, signaling the bias inherent in many studies. Just as Americans have come to distrust any study about smoking funded by the tobacco industry, I found that many health tests are funded and supported by oil companies, environmental groups, and grants from universities or labs dependent on donors for their livelihood. In the search for truth, one cannot help but become a bit jaded by the influence money wields on public health issues. It became apparent to me that objectivity and public welfare are only distantly related.

Also obvious was that common sense, if indeed it still exists, is at times the best barometer when making decisions about one's own health. The scientists I spoke with were from both sides of the belief spectrum, and all—Brockovich's experts, the city's specialists, the public entities—left me convinced of their sincerity to flesh out the truth, but whose truth was truth? Although we are all trained to believe science is exact, there is subjectivity swirled heavily throughout the mix. I imagine this is why a parent or citizen must ultimately rely on his or her own common sense to discern the safety of their surroundings. Whose agenda is being served and how does it impact the greater good? Discovering those answers takes a great deal of investigation and time, and most parents are sorely lacking in both.

Epidemiologist Dr. Wendy Cozen explained that in the last few years, certain factors have become generally accepted as causes of disease. That smoking and asbestos show direct links to cancer is a conclusion no one would argue any longer. Other issues are not so black and white and evidence exists on both sides to create doubt in even the most reasonable people. One thing no one can doubt is the determination of every reasonable parent to protect the health and safety of their children. However, without knowledge, how can accurate decisions be discerned?

According to Cozen, certain diseases are on the rise in children. Some may be universal, like diabetes, and related to lifestyle and genetics in lieu of environment. Others will show prevalence in a certain area, like asthma in the Long Beach corridor outside Los Angeles. Asthma affects the lungs and tests have shown it may be directly related to a rise in air particulates like benzene and other volatile organic compounds near the L.A. Port and the 710 Freeway. Tests have shown the seventeen or so ships that reach the port each day pollute more than the over three hundred oil-producing facilities in the L.A. Basin combined. It would be difficult not to notice the air near Long Beach. Anyone who has driven the 710 Freeway has seen for themselves the mass of trucks exploding benzene particulates into the air. Witnessing this cloud of black hovering overhead, can there be any doubt the air is unhealthy to breathe?

This is an example of the obvious effects of pollution and should serve as a warning to parents to keep their children as far away from such an unhealthy environment as possible. But do all families heed the warning? Is it always possible for them to do so? No, and perhaps that is why such environmentally linked diseases are on the rise. Living near a freeway creates higher risk and yet many people buy homes near freeways, chemical plants, and corporations on a daily basis. Some may check with authorities on the safety; others may not. When they do they may receive confusing conclusions, so how is it possible to decide with confidence?

The second problem citizens face is the reality that government paces itself like a turtle, while pollution runs like a hare. As new health guidelines are determined in an attempt to clean the air and environment, the period between the discovery, discussion, compromise, passage, and implementation can be years. In the time between, all are breathing levels of toxins we have now determined unsafe.

Another factor in solving health problems is the inconsistency of the testing. Whether pertaining to air, soil, or water, in studying the newest problems we face, every result has its opposite in scientific research. How is it possible to effect legislation to regulate issues when no clear answers exist? Or when they do, it takes years to change the safety standards? Or when legislators rely on polluting companies to fund their election war chests?

It is also incredibly difficult to discern fact from fiction when plaintiffs and defendants fund experts. Money changing hands alters the dynamic and compromises the integrity of testimony or conclusions offered by paid scientists. Some of these expert witnesses offered experimental evidence not yet widely verified. I offer no judgment about the validity of their opinions but chose to rely on widespread scientific methodology and the ultimate determination of the court as it pertains to this case. No journalist could ignore the results and conclusions of the federally and state-mandated agencies in charge of oversight without significant, reliable evidence to the contrary.

With hidden agendas clouding an already murky issue, we are bombarded daily with frightening scenarios about New York flooding under the weight of global warming, polar bears becoming extinct, and Arctic icecaps melting and drifting into our backyards like the sludge from a mudslide in Los Angeles. How much is truth and how much is designed to line the pockets of "greenscammers"? With so much green involved, perhaps we need to question the green message. The term "tree huggers" was once used to describe those who valued nature. This did not lack virtue, nor was it profitable. Not at first. In fact, in those days, the connotation was negative in nature. As tree huggers aged, however, some became aware there is opportunity for gold in the green.

It is also ironic, and perhaps amusing, that many of the law firms and "green" generals that battle these egregious environmental issues fly private jets and make tons of money exploiting these issues. The hypocrisy is staggering and perhaps that is why situations like Beverly Hills arise. We need to be informed and highly skeptical of anyone making health claims because for every test there may exist an opposite result. We also need to be aware that what exists as true today may change tomorrow and links may be established that furnish new evidence of dangers and problems.

Government agencies are understaffed, overworked, and operate under an enormous burden. They are forced to prioritize cases and focus their attention on the most egregious and widespread polluters. The Air Quality Management District, for example, does not test regularly or voluntarily at every oil facility in Los Angeles. According to Sam Atwood, "How would it be possible to check every facility when there are 28,000 to regulate in Southern California? You focus on the largest facilities and oil refineries. For example, we have an inspector at the refineries on a daily basis and prioritize the largest polluters."

Atwood says all complaints are addressed and if there is an odor problem, the AQMD is authorized to issue a citation of odor nuisances. They also have special monitoring programs for high schools, day cares, and senior facilities. "If we become concerned there is a health risk, air monitoring is implemented and we have equipment at the site for weeks, months, or a year." For major facilities the goal is to conduct yearly inspections.

The enormous task these agencies face makes it imperative for communities to self-monitor and seek objective help on environmental problems. Relying on all five senses and common sense should be the goal. Simply looking for spillage, noxious odors, or anything out of the ordinary health-wise can be the clue necessary to initiate action and prevent the escalation of a problem.

If an agency validates a community's suspicions but fails to act, citizens' best recourse may ultimately be the press. Neither corporate nor civil polluters desire publicity for their bad behavior. Following the *Valdez* oil spill, people drove by Exxon gas stations, and BP will take years to recover, if ever, from the Gulf oil spill. The TV ads portraying sincere efforts to clean up the coast and help the victims are clearly the public relations war they intend to wage to "fix" their image. The budgets companies allocate to public relations speak volumes about how much they value their public image. Bad publicity can become a valuable weapon for the individual, ensuring that the appropriate agencies move quickly to correct health hazards. Yet, too often the public forgets this crucial piece of the puzzle.

Journalists are charged with uncovering information daily and possess the knowledge to acquire public records. They often acquire records and information before it can be covered up, destroyed, or legally protected as work product. Whereas trial lawyers are ignited by a gigantic settlement, most reporters, especially those who consider themselves to be investigative-oriented, are impassioned by a potential pollution story.

No one should discount the effectiveness of community papers. Whereas a large newspaper must budget resources and reporters, a community paper is the advocate closest to the situation. Major news outlets may also be owned by large conglomerates that have financial ties to the very people they are investigating. Oftentimes, as in Beverly Hills, reporters have far greater access to the players and can attain information an outsider would not be aware is available.

One caveat regarding media reporting is that many outlets tend to give credibility to statements made by high-profile players because they garner attention and promote greater readership. This poses a problem when the purveyors of these facts, although they can get a great table in an L.A. restaurant, are not capable of understanding or disseminating true science. Therefore, serious citizens with environmental concerns should be cautious about both the message and the messenger. It is interesting to note that despite the large number of celebrity alumni Beverly Hills High boasts, I never received a call or question from these well-known individuals.

While reporting alleged polluters to the media or to government agencies may serve to ameliorate or even stop the violations, one highly effective way communities can safeguard against problems is prevention. A unified group of parents, PTA members, businesspeople, or representatives from the local political scene may anticipate and address issues concerning their area before negative situations arise. Once yearly an impartial environmental expert—an expert within the community may be far better than hiring an outside source—should be called to survey any potential health issues. This safety check should encompass air quality, soil gases, and water. A problem can be determined by comparing figures from year to year. Such constant monitoring makes determining where polluters are based and the source of changes much easier. It is surprising how often this simple step is overlooked until it is too late. Costs for communities who uncover a potential problem should be covered within school or city budgets, especially if facilities like oil wells exist near public entities.

A good proactive policy may be to invite members of local

corporations to speak at town hall meetings and discuss ways they plan to address any potential environmental problems. It is not unusual today for companies to install safeguards and measures to deflect pollution as a matter of course and regulation. Updates on these repairs and upgrades should be noted.

Citizens should start a community environmental watch group. Just as neighborhood watch has helped increase awareness, an SOK (Save Our Kids) group can help stop pollution.

Products like the MiniRAE 3000, a hand-held unit for VOC measurement, provide detection below 1 ppb. At a cost of approximately $2,000 it is accessible to individuals and organizations. This is only one example of the many options available to the public within a wide price range.

Keeping a list of relevant agencies is a fast, easy way to ensure help and good advice is close at hand. It also eliminates any delays in reaching the appropriate entity when and if a troubling situation occurs.

Citizens can organize bake sales and other fundraisers to generate money to "green" the public areas. Contests between schools could encourage new ideas for making the community cleaner.

Committees should look into adding solar panels to public schools and municipal buildings and encourage the local government to foster initiatives for the business community to go solar. Grants are available for these "green" changes and it is often cost-effective as well.

Many cities offer grants to help fund monitoring by citizen groups, and a search of federal grants to fund community environmental groups will pull up thousands of responses on the Internet. Among the many informative resources on the Internet are Global Community Monitor's Bucket Brigade, Coming Clean's Community Monitoring Handbook, and the

EPA's Community Service Projects page. All provide valuable tools for self-monitoring.

Regulatory agencies keep information about manufacturing plants in the local community. With a phone call to verify their history and violations, concerned citizens can create a list of those businesses that are cooperative and those that are not, thereby acquiring a clear picture of where more oversight is necessary. Establishing a partnership with local businesses may go a long way toward solving problems that could later arise.

Becoming environmentally informed is sometimes as simple as awareness. The following are suggestions for communities and individuals to promote greener values.

Community Green Awards are one way to encourage corporations and businesses in your area to be a "good environmental team player." Public relations are a big part of any company strategy and a public pat on the back is positive incentive. Green Awards can be given through or in concert with the local newspaper, PTA, city, chamber of commerce, or local environmental groups. There should be as much visibility for these awards as possible. The company should receive special perks in the area, a picture in the newspaper, a mention at city council or perhaps at a local fair, signs in stores, and blurbs in local newsletters. Whatever a community can do to reward the corporation or business will go a long way toward informing these companies that residents support those who support their environment. These actions also send the important message that the community is casting a watchful environmental eye.

There are numerous groups across the country that address issues citizens face if threatened with pollution or dangerous chemicals in their community. Offering information on successful ways to combat violators, watchdog organizations like the Blue Ridge Environmental Defense League (BREDL) were created to help battle polluters. Their effectiveness can be seen in how they successfully opposed an asphalt plant in Alamance County, North Carolina, in 2007. Locals founded Be Safe Not Sorry (BSNS) and joined with BREDL to organize public meetings and publicity to prevent the company from building their proposed plant. Through their efforts, they were able to pass the Alamance County High Impact Land Uses/Polluting Industries Ordinance, which blocks asphalt plants and other polluters. Today, BSNS is still diligent about overseeing the area and attends meetings to ensure polluters are thwarted in the earliest stages.

Campaigns and public awareness are key in preventing problems before they take hold, and there is evidence throughout the country that one person can stimulate that change. Heal the Bay in Santa Monica, California, is a perfect example of how a community can positively impact the environment. Heal the Bay was formed when, in the 1980s, sewage spills into the bay forced beach closures. Local activists banded together and organizing a group urging the city to clean up. Inspired by its founder, Dorothy Green, others were motivated to join the cause and the group blossomed. Advocates readily admit that Green's passion attracted the attorneys, professors, entertainers, and environmental leaders capable of inspiring others.

In an interview with Heal the Bay executive director Dr. Mark Gold, he praised the citizens for their ideals and goals: "This is a city of progressive residents, staff, and a city council who are so very creative and willing to try and fail. Most cities aren't willing to do that, but instead do the safe thing. Santa Monica will try new experiments and some work, some don't."

Innovative programs like Heal the Bay have been highly

effective at repairing the ravages to Santa Monica Bay. "I am proudest of the fact that someone would be hard pressed to find anyone who thinks the bay is as polluted today as it was twenty years ago. Changes in the water quality and ecology of the bay have been dramatic."

Although environmental causes can prove frustrating when tracking a problem's progress for twenty years, Gold remains optimistic and adamant Heal the Bay's original mission still holds true. "I will not be satisfied until the bay is completely free of pollution and all the natural resources are protected. Rainstorms impact water quality on the beaches and in the bay and we have barely scratched the surface in twenty years, even with regulatory progress. The only way to improve the problem would be a total change in waste disposal behavior as a city." While traffic and a lack of green space exacerbates the problem, Gold insists personal options such as littering, cleaning up after pets, assuring no oil leaks from cars, properly disposing of antifreeze, composting, and recycling programs by both business and residents have a significant effect on pollution levels.

Gold continues, "The Santa Monica beaches represent the California lifestyle. The importance of the area as a destination and escape played a large role in igniting passion to preserve a way of life vital to all Californians."

He notes that smaller cities have an advantage in their ability to act. "In large cities, if something goes wrong the mayor is blamed. In smaller cities where mayors are not elected but rotate, they are not under a microscope and have less accountability."

While individual cities have initiated various programs to enhance air and water quality, many of the serious problems facing residents lie in the hands of federally operated agencies and guidelines, oftentimes tying the hands of local advocates. Despite roadblocks, many have created successful programs to improve quality of living standards.

While environmental groups and local leaders work at the regional and statewide levels, there are many successful and recommended strategies that can be enacted on the personal level to help maintain a clean community environment. Individuals can talk to the school district about replacing diesel buses with buses powered by cleaner fuels like natural gas, fuel cells, or electricity. Taking the train or bus when possible, carpooling, and encouraging children to employ low-pollution transportation like bikes or roller skates, combined with regular emission checkups for the family car, also cut emissions with little effort. Driving less and walking more, taking lunch to work or walking to lunch if possible, riding a bike and encouraging others to do the same, and urging businesses to install modern bike racks for employees may decrease drivers as well. Holding conference calls or computer meetings instead of attending in-person can also help reduce air pollution.

Do not top off your tank, and be sure to wait before removing the nozzle, as fuel spillage adds to air pollution. Opt for water-based paints and cleaning products, reduce energy consumption, and forego use of wood stoves and fireplaces on days when air quality is poor. When possible, avoid using leaf blowers and other dust-producing equipment. Use electric lawnmowers or push lawnmowers, which provide the added benefit of adding some exercise to your routine.

Schedule speakers in schools to talk with students about ways to reduce pollution. Local cable shows dedicated to informing local residents about the environment are also highly beneficial for disseminating information. Not everything is possible in all areas, but many strategies can be successfully implemented in your community.

Numerous organizations throughout the country are highly effective and can be called in to help individuals make a difference. The following are a few that specialize in specific areas of concern.

American Forests Global ReLeaf campaign protects trees and forests through tree planting to save energy, protect wildlife, and clean the air and water. 910 17th Street NW, Suite 600, Washington, D.C., 20006, (800) 368-5748, www.amfor.org.

American Rivers' goal is to restore America's waterways, revitalize urban rivers, protect fish and wildlife, and fight pollution. 1025 Vermont Avenue NW, Suite 720, Washington, D.C., 20005, (800) 296-6900, www.amrivers.org.

Beyond Pesticides/National Coalition Against the Misuse of Pesticides is an information clearinghouse on environmental pesticide poisoning, toxic hazards, and non-chemical alternative pest control. 701 E Street SE, Washington, D.C., 20003, (202) 543-5450, www.beyondpesticides.org.

Center for Health, Environment and Justice helps protect families from environmental toxic chemicals. PO Box 6806, Falls Church, VA, 22040, (703) 237-2249, www.chej.org.

The Annual Coastal Cleanup promotes marine sanctuaries and conserves fisheries. 1725 DeSales Street NW, Suite 600, Washington, D.C., 20036, (202) 429-5609, www.cmc-ocean.org.

Clean Water Fund is a neighborhood-based education and action program for clean water, pollution prevention, and resource conservation. 4455 Connecticut Avenue NW, Suite A300, Washington, D.C., 20008-2328, (202) 895-0432, www.cleanwaterfund.org.

The Conservation Fund protects wetlands, wildlife habitat, and open space. 1800 North Kent Street, Suite 1120, Arlington,

VA, 22209, (703) 525-6300, www.conservationfund.org.

Defenders of Wildlife are dedicated to habitat protection and prevention of species extinction through innovative leadership. Wildlife protection programs include Northern Rockies grizzly recovery, wolf restoration, and wildcat, bird, marine wildlife, and dolphin protection. 1101 14th Street NW, Suite 1400, Washington, D.C., 20005, (202) 682-9400, www.defenders.org.

Earth Day Network holds annual campaigns and organizes groups worldwide to promote social justice, sustainability, and a healthy environment. 91 Marion Street, Seattle, WA, 98104, (206) 264-0114, www.earthday.net.

Earthjustice Legal Defense Fund, formerly the Sierra Club Legal Defense Fund, provides free legal representation to citizen groups to enforce environmental laws and protect wildlife, natural resources, and people. 180 Montgomery Street, Suite 1400, San Francisco, CA, 94104, (415) 627-6700, www.earthjustice.org.

Environmental and Energy Study Institute develops and promotes policy related to climate change, clean air, energy efficiency and renewable energy technologies, transportation, and sprawl. They provide education, advocacy, and coalition building. 122 C Street NW, Suite 700, Washington, D.C., 20001, (202) 628-1400, www.eesi.org.

The Environmental Defense Fund promotes sustainable, just solutions to complex environmental problems. They focus on biodiversity, climate, health, and oceans. 257 Park Avenue South, New York, NY, 10010, (800) 684-3322, www.edf.org.

The Environmental Justice Foundation is benefitting communities of color through organizing, educating, and training. 310 8th Street, #309, Oakland, CA, 94607, (510) 834-8920, www.ejfoundation.org.

Friends of the Earth empower citizen action and expose wasteful federal spending and tax subsidies for corporate polluters. 1025 Vermont Avenue NW, Suite 300, Washington, D.C., 20005, (202) 783-7400, www.foe.org.

INFORM, Inc. is focused on clean air and reducing solid and toxic waste. They assist communities, businesses, and policymakers in finding constructive solutions. 120 Wall Street, 16th Floor, New York, NY, 10005-4001, (212) 361-2400, www.informinc.org.

Izaak Walton League of America preserves the legacy of the American outdoors, focusing on wildlife, habitat, clean air, and water. They offer watershed protection, energy efficiency, sustainable agriculture, and forestry. 707 Conservation Lane, Gaithersburg, MD, 20878, (800) IKE-LINE, www.iwla.org.

Land Trust Alliance assists local land trusts and conservationists in preserving habitats, parks, trails, and green space. It provides essential information, training, networking, and policy advocacy. 1319 F Street NW, Suite 501, Washington, D.C., 20004, (202) 638-4725, www.lta.org.

National Audubon Society exists to protect wildlife, birds, and habitat on national and local levels through education, citizen activism, and field science. There are 518 chapters, more than 100 wildlife sanctuaries, and over 500,000 teachers and children reached every year. 700 Broadway, New York, NY, 10003, (212) 979-3000, www.audubon.org.

The National Parks and Conservation Association works across America to preserve national parks, promote new parks, protect endangered wildlife and cultural sites, and defend against such issues as pollution, inappropriate development, and overcrowding. 1776 Massachusetts Avenue NW, Suite 200, Washington, D.C., 20036, (800) NAT-PARK, www.npca.org.

National Wildlife Federation protects wildlife and natural habitats and educates with *Ranger Rick,* among other publications. 8925 Leesburg Pike, Vienna, VA, 22184, (800) 332-4949, x4016, www.nwf.org.

The Nature Conservancy purchased and protects over 10 million acres of rainforests, wetlands, prairies, mountains, and coastline. 4245 North Fairfax Drive, Suite 100, Arlington, VA, 22203-1606, (703) 841-5300, www.tnc.org.

Rails-to-Trails Conservancy is a national organization working to convert thousands of miles of unused railways into trails for pedestrians, bicyclists, hikers, skaters, horseback riders, cross-country skiers, and naturalists. 1100 17th Street NW, 10th Floor, Washington, D.C., 20036, (202) 331-9696, www.railstotrails.org.

Scenic America protects America's natural beauty and special places and fights billboard blight. 801 Pennsylvania Avenue, SE, Suite 300, Washington, D.C., 20003, (202) 543-6200, www.scenic.org.

Student Conservation Association is the nation's leading service to nature organization. PO Box 550, Route 12A, River Road, Charleston, NH, 03603, (603) 543-1700, www.sca-inc.org.

Surfrider Foundation is a nonprofit international environmental organization focused on protection of beaches through conservation, activism, research, and education. 122 South El Camino Real, #67, San Clemente, CA, 92672, (800) 743-SURF, www.surfrider.org.

Trust for Public Land has converted over a million acres of vacant lots and other land into urban gardens and public parks. 116 New Montgomery Street, 4th Floor, San Francisco, CA, 94105, (800) 714-LAND, www.tpl.org.

U.S. PIRG Education Fund works with citizens to protect clean air and water, conserve natural resources, and prevent global warming. 218 D Street SE, Washington, D.C., 20003, (202) 546-9707, www.pirg.org.

The Wilderness Society is dedicated to the lasting protection of spectacular American wilderness in parks, rivers, forests, deserts, and shorelines. 900 17th Street NW, Washington, D.C., 20006, (800) THE-WILD, www.wilderness.org.

Clean Water Action, Washington, D.C., provides education and help for community groups. (202) 895-0420, www.cleanwateractions.org.

Communities Concerned about Corporations works with communities and industries on Zero Discharge projects. 5401 42nd Avenue, Hyattsville, MD, 20781, (301) 779-1000.

Ecological Consultants for the Public Interest is a national, nonprofit, foundation-supported consulting firm formed to provide citizens with professional services to help them understand, address, and remediate environmental problems. 1942 Broadway, Boulder, CO, 80302, (303) 938-3773, www.cqs.com/ecpi.htm.

Greenpeace, USA, Washington, D.C. provides a huge array of educational materials and news about pollution and takes part in direct action and protest against polluters. www.greenpeace.org.

Organic Consumers Association is an online, grassroots nonprofit public interest organization campaigning for health, justice, and sustainability. 3547 Haines Road, Duluth, MN, 55811, (218) 726-1443, www.organicconsumers.org.

Pesticide Action Network North America, at www.panna.org, is a nonprofit citizen-based non-government organization that advocates adoption of ecologically sound practices in lieu of pesticide use. The newly discovered and constantly changing dangers of pesticides should be high on the list of any community environmental action group.

These organizations are a small example of the vast number of groups fighting for a cleaner environment. Using your computer and a search engine or picking up the phone can instantly empower any individual or group seeking help.

14

Informing the Individual

Whenever the people are well-informed, they can be trusted with their own government.

—Thomas Jefferson

The world is changing. Somewhere along the way, while we were looking for a good lease on our car, trying to figure out how to use a Bluetooth, and hiring personal trainers to whip us into shape, we evolved. Baby Boomers developed an environmental conscience with a desire to know more than just who was picking our lettuce; we wanted to know how it was grown, what chemicals were used, and how it was harvested. The generation that thought Howdy Doody was high-tech and Nestle made the very best chocolate suddenly discovered words like trans fats, e. coli, benzene, and chromium six. These substances were purported to be hindering our ability to live long and productive lives. This new awakening inspires us to down vitamins like M&Ms and discuss herbal supplements the way we once discussed Elvis's latest record. While tooling around town in a Prius, drivers display more smugness per mile than any Porsche Turbo ever delivered. Our shopping carts are filled with organic fruits and vegetables and designer coffees. Shopping farmers' markets and donating heavily to Darfur relief are priorities.

The Baby Boomers have achieved metamorphosis and seek answers to questions they never knew existed. How is this product made? What's used in production? Where was it produced and how healthy are the workers? What is the shelf life, ingredients, lifespan, and how will its afterlife affect our environment? What is the best way to teach our children to reduce their carbon footprint? Our products have biographies and we want to know their history so that we can make greener judgments. Label reading has become as much a part of our daily existence as yoga and the Internet. Green is no longer a color Kermit finds it difficult to be, but a lifestyle. Papers are recycled, products are biodegradable, and we are entering new eco-friendly worlds even Rod Serling couldn't have imagined.

Suddenly our children and grandchildren are conversing with us about Styrofoam bans in their schools and global warming. They have become the egg teaching the chickens and in our desire to live longer and healthier lives we have learned the language and embraced the concept. We are adamant our garbage not poison people, the oceans are clean, and transporting food to market is safe, efficient, and non-polluting.

Despite all this new awareness, pollution still hits us with that one-two punch every time our back is turned. Oil spills, sewage leaks, and fish with weird and scary diseases are showing up where we routinely take a morning dip. Although many are secure and happy in this new "green" lifestyle, others doubt the veracity of linking illness to the barrage of chemicals we are exposed to each day. Tests are routinely done and often present conflicting results. Who is to be believed and how can a concerned parent and community member discern truth from fiction? How do we make intelligent decisions about our environment as it impacts our ability to live in an enlightened society balancing both progress and healthy lifestyles? If we are going to coexist with nature and technology, can we reconcile the two?

Sadly, it isn't an easy task. Although there are numerous proven toxins with an undeniable link to illness, it would be impossible to test the combined effects of the army of potentially harmful substances that greet an average person each day. Nevertheless, it is an investigative feat worth pursuing, and fortunately there are numerous agencies and reports available to aid in the search.

Since we all do our fair share of breathing, perhaps air is a good place to begin. Californians and other big-city dwellers are no strangers to multicolored air. Far from invisible, it hovers over our cities like a giant reddish-brown cloak, marking our cars, lawn furniture, and foliage. Most people are unaware that components of California's colored air include a mixture of H_2O, polluted particulates, and disintegrating rubber, a.k.a. tires.

Each day the over 11 million cars in the L.A. area crowd the 405 Freeway seeking an exit and hoping for a speedy arrival at their destination. Each car possesses a minimum of four tires, and big rigs sport more. The lifespan of the American tire is four years. Do the math. This rubber dust becomes part of our atmosphere, dropping onto us and our possessions as well as into our water supply and drains. More importantly, we inhale it into our lungs. Recently South Coast Air Quality officials in Denver reported a study concluding that "latex in road dust produced as vehicle tires wear is probably responsible for an increase in asthma attacks and asthma-related deaths in the United States during the last decade. Road dust, including tiny bits of tire wear, can account for up to 50 percent of particulate pollution in urban areas." Another study confirmed the presence of extractable latex antigens from rubber tire fragments. Results concluded, "The adjuvant and sensitizing effects of airborne latex could contribute, through direct and indirect mechanisms, to the increase in both latex sensitization and asthma. The impact of these particles should be considered in the issue of morbidity and mortality rates associated with respiratory diseases and air pollution."

When asked if there is a solution to this dilemma, AQMD spokesmen are silent. After all, tires are a way of life. We can't drive very far without them. Quite simply, until our jet packs are ready for consumer use, we are obliged to speed along the highway in our motor-driven vehicles, spewing benzene and worn rubber particulates into the environment. It's an unfortunate fact of life to be sure, but perhaps it's time to focus on the total picture. Look at the complete car, the entire rubber-spewing enchilada. How can we effectively eliminate tire particulates from our environmental footprint? This seems to be a question that begs the consistent answer: drive less, walk more, use mass transit, or choke.

As if it's not bad enough that tires spew their particles through the air we breathe, getting rid of them also seems to be a monumental task. California generates more than 41 million waste tires annually. Despite recycling 75 percent, the remaining waste tires constitute a 10-million-tire stockpile yearly. Two of California's worst man-made environmental disasters were unpermitted, multimillion-dollar tire collections that resulted in massive tire fires that put the public, land, air, and area water supply at serious risk.

What can consumers do to prevent the problem? Are tires a small part of the air quality problem? They are certainly part of the equation and one that deserves a community's attention. Using longer lasting tires, retreading used tires, disposing properly of old tires, and using products composed of recycled rubber are a few of the suggestions available at websites like Earth 911.

Another critical component of air problems is pesticides. Recent studies have shown a direct link between health issues and the use of organophosphate pesticides. A study published in *Pediatrics* "demonstrates a link between Attention Deficit Hyperactive Disorder and organophosphate pesticides." The Harvard-based study, "Attention-Deficit/Hyperactivity Disorder and Urinary Metabolites of Organophosphate Pesticides," found a strong correlation between the level of pesticides detected in the urine of children and the condition known as attention deficit hyperactivity disorder. Researchers concluded, "These findings support the hypothesis that organophosphate exposure, at levels common among US children, may contribute to ADHD prevalence. Prospective studies are needed to establish whether this association is causal."

Studies show that "organophosphate pesticides account for about half of the insecticides used in the United States and act by interfering with the transmission of signals in the nervous systems of both insects and humans, when exposed in high enough amounts." The Centers for Disease Control and Prevention warns that eating foods that have been sprayed with organophosphates can affect an individual's health.

A lawsuit filed in 2008 to ban the most egregious of these pesticides has not yet been resolved. However, there are numerous organic pesticides on the market that are natural and non-evasive. There are multiple resources available to help make your home pesticide free.

I would be remiss if I failed to address one of the simplest ways to cut down on air problems. Cows. The world's penchant for cheeseburgers and a good steak is a major component of methane issues in the environment. The astronomical numbers displayed on every McDonald's sign is proof positive there is a high demand for meat among the population. A United Nations report in 2006 cited, "The release of methane into the atmosphere is a major problem. According to the UN Food and Agriculture Organisation [FAO], farm animals are responsible for 18 per cent of total greenhouse gas emissions."

Although there are studies underway to address these problems, the Swiss have discovered that adding tannins and flax seed to hay may reduce these emissions. There is also a simpler way to help; cutting back on meat consumption may be the easiest fix. Adding a salmon meal to your diet once a week is better for your health and the Earth's as well. Eating a salad in lieu of a steak will produce a cleaner and safer environment for yourself and your community.

The following is a list of websites that furnish information about air quality and environmental issues and studies. They are a helpful source, providing updates on the newest information for your community and your children. Some are government sponsored, some privately funded by various organizations and groups. These sites furnish information about upcoming health, safety, and environmental meetings in your area. PTA and neighborhood groups might find it helpful to appoint a rotating committee of members to do monthly checks on favorite sites and report back to the membership on the latest findings.

The GoodGuide at www.goodguide.com rates products and includes information on food safety and health for children and their parents.

The Environmental Protection Agency has a special web page for parents and students at www.epa.gov/highschool/health.htm. It is designed to address environmental health and safety problems and solutions.

Facts and figures about the ozone can be found at www.epa.gov/oar/oaqps/gooduphigh.

Those concerned about the ultraviolet (UV) index and what they can do to minimize the harmful effects of overexposure or who are interested in the current UV index for their zip code can find the information at www.epa.gov/sunwise/uvindex.html.

The American Lung Association's "State of the Air" report at www.stateoftheair.org/ provides information about air quality in local communities.

For information on asthma and upper respiratory illnesses, visit the EPA's Asthma page at www.epa.gov/asthma.

Read about the risks of environmental tobacco smoke and find links to research studies about the issue at www.epa.gov/smokefree/healtheffects.html.

Information on secondhand smoke is available through the EPA at www.epa.gov/smokefree/healtheffects.html.

The EPA, NOAA, and NPS, in concert with tribal, state, and local agencies, developed the AIRNow website to provide the public with easy access to national air quality information. AIRNow lists up-to-the-minute information about air pollution in the community, including maps, forecasts, and health effects at http://airnow.gov.

The EPA provides basic facts about pollutants found inside our buildings and homes at The Inside Story: A Guide to Indoor Air Quality, www.epa.gov/iaq/pubs/insidest.html.

The National Institute for Environmental Health Sciences' website, www.niehs.nih.gov, is a site for students, teachers, and scientists and covers environmental health information, activities, jobs, and developmental opportunities.

The Green Flag Program at www.greenflagschools.org helps schools provide healthier spaces for children and teaches students about the school's environment.

The EPA's Healthy School Environments, www.cfpub.epa. gov/schools/index.cfm, is a resource designed to help facility managers, school administrators, architects, design engineers, school nurses, parents, teachers, and staff address environmental health issues in schools.

For access to the laws that protect the air, the EPA provides a simple guide at www.epa.gov/air/caa/peg/understand.html.

The Center for Innovative Engineering and Science Education hosts an interactive and fun educational website at www. k12science.org/curriculum/airproj that teaches grades 6-12 about air pollution.

The EPA offers the Environmental Kids Club page at www. epa.gov/kids/ with a variety of environmental topics presented in an easily understandable manner for children.

There is a wealth of links to fun, creative, and informative environmental websites for children at eartheasy.com/ blog/2009/03/environmental-websites-for-kids/.

FT Exploring, an educational site available at www.ftex ploring.com, is geared toward educators teaching the better use of energy.

EekoWorld at http://pbskids.org/eekoworld/ is a PBS website that teaches children aged six to nine years how to help care for the earth. It features animated characters, games, and activities to educate kids about ecosystems and pollution. Children are offered the opportunity to build an "EekoCreature" and help it overcome environmental problems.

Nature Challenge for Kids at www.davidsuzuki.org/kids/

is sponsored by the David Suzuki Foundation. It provides ten simple ways to protect nature, followed by four challenge activities offering hands-on experience with the natural world. There is also a "Cool Links" page that connects kids to other environmental websites.

A wildlife adoption center is available at www.kidsplanet.org.

Eco-Kids at www.ecokids.ca/pub/index.cfm is Earth Day Canada's environmental education program. Designed to be interactive and fun and provide educational games and activities, the website encourages children "to form their own opinions, make decisions, get involved and understand the impact their own actions have on the environment."

The National Resources Defense Council's Green Squad at www.nrdc.org/greensauad/ helps kids identify and solve environmental problems. The colorful virtual schoolroom allows users to navigate and locate potential hazards.

The Canadian Government's Big Blue Bus, at www.dfo mpo.gc.ca/canwaters-eauxcan/bbb-lgb/index_e.asp, is designed for children aged eight to sixteen, with a club for kids under seven. Cartoon characters present kids with games and activities to learn about "all things watery."

The Wildlife Conservation Society's website at www.kids gowild.org is filled with animal facts and information about environmental issues.

The U.S. Department of Energy has created, among other child-directed activities, Roofus' Home at www.eere.energy.gov/kids/. A dog named Roofus, an expert on solar energy and energy efficiency, guides visitors through his energy smart house.

Planet Slayer, www.planetslayer.com, offers games like "Greena, the Worrier Princess," an animated Australian teenager with a sense of purpose to save the earth.

The United Nations offers an environmental magazine for

young people at www.unep.org/tunza/children/. The articles
are written for teens by teens around the world.

Environmental Education for Kids or EEK!, an online
magazine for grades four to eight, contains articles and activities about animals, plants and environmental issues at www.
dnr.state.wi.us/eek/.

Field Trip Earth is a site where children can travel the world
via interviews. At www.fieldtripearth.org/ there are discussions, essays, and educator resources. The site has a "Choose
a Field Trip" page, with an airplane cursor that allows kids to
select a wildlife project to visit.

Children of the Earth United, www.childrenoftheearth.org/,
promotes understanding and respect for the earth and informs
children about the environmental effects of their actions.

Flying WILD, www.flyingwild.org/, teaches children about
birds and wild animals. It is an initiative of the Council for
Environmental Education's Project WILD program.

Treetures at www.treetures.com/Meet1.htm is a colorful,
fun site for kids. The "Treetures" are tiny guardians of the
forest who lead children down the website trail using acorns
to teach about trees and the environment. Kids can send a
"TreeMail" message to their favorite character.

WebRangers, www.webrangers.us/, is the National Park
Service's site for kids of all ages. There are activities for three
age groups (six and up, ten and up, thirteen and up) including puzzles, games, and activities designed to educate children
about nature.

Bringing a virtual natural world into the classroom, Earth
Matters 4 Kids, www.earthmatters4kids.org/main.html, com-
bines science with basic environmental principles for teachers, students (K-6), and community members.

Sustainable Environment for Quality of Life at Centralina

Council of Governments, www.seql.org/100ways.cfm, suggests 100 ways to save the environment.

The National Institutes of Health, www.nih.gov/, is a great resource for the latest tests and information concerning health issues.

Searching Internet organizations that protect the environment will provide numerous up-to-date sites as well as information. Perhaps a list of these organizations and websites can be included in the PTA or local environmental group newsletter each month.

15

The Need for Personal Accountability

All truth passes through three stages. First, it is ridiculed.
Second, it is violently opposed. Third, it is accepted as being
self-evident.

—Arthur Schopenhauer

It was quite a surprise that after wracking my brain on
numerous occasions to create a storyline for my first literary
endeavor—one that would cause the pipe-smoking, suede-
elbow-patched among us to rise from their burgundy leather
wing chairs and shout "Brava!"—I stumbled headfirst into
Erin Brockovich, oil wells, and all the fun tort law offers. Ide-
alism is something I believed faded with age, like muscle tone,
and I was as shocked as could be to learn I still possessed
an abundant supply of it. While Erin was afforded the royal
treatment by the established media giants, I found myself driving the Little Engine That Could uphill. After all, why would
anyone take a newspaper that covered luncheons, charity
events, and openings on Rodeo Drive seriously? Sneaking a
truckload of dynamite filled with truth in the backdoor made
the experience all the more fun and rewarding.

Events of the Beverly Hills versus Erin Brockovich oil well

lawsuit story unraveled as an urban cautionary tale replete with a colorful cast of characters, but the hero of this tale is the message. Lessons learned should resonate with a clear and truthful ring to serve as a warning to parents and communities across America to protect the health of their children and citizens, a wake-up call to reject those who would exploit the illness and suffering of others as a steppingstone to wealth, fame, and fortune. Until we stop politicizing the health and welfare of our children, these types of events will continue to occur with regularity. Masking truths and padding the pockets of lawyers and environmental crusaders who exploit these deeds for their own benefit will continue to be the norm. "Greenscam" has become the new green agenda and a means to "sexy up" and direct people away from the real problems and dangerous side effects inherent in an industrial society.

Each community should join together to strengthen the wellness fabric of America. Citizens can stand up and take control of their own destinies once more, and it begins at home. If a grocery or retailer in your neighborhood is selling products from companies that pollute or poison, boycott. Organizing efforts within PTA and community groups to pressure those companies that pollute or buy products from countries that do not enforce safety and industry standards will go a long way toward stopping the problem. Of all the weapons Americans possess, the mighty dollar is the most powerful in its arsenal. Nothing will get the attention of a company that trades in poison as quickly as withdrawing money from their bottom line.

Empowering your neighbors to act will make all the difference to the health and welfare of children and families. No shipment from countries that regularly ignore health standards should cross the threshold into the United States. This lack of oversight and control is reckless and dangerous. Leaflets, newsletters, and updates at PTA and city council meetings, and local organizations can inform parents regarding harmful polluters. Working together also serves to unify and create a strong community-building agenda that helps families in a multitude of ways.

Although Beverly Hills prevailed legally, the ill effects remain a painful reminder of what can happen when citizens become complacent about the air they breathe. Questions ultimately asked there need to be asked by every community with industrial facilities within their borders. I believe Venoco will be successful in future lease negotiations with Beverly Hills. My opinion is based on my perception that parents have stopped paying attention, and when government entities are left to their own devices, the public is shortchanged. The point of this book is not to prove whether or not a problem existed, but rather to point out that too many do and go unnoticed until harm is already done. That parents and communities can avoid the pitfalls of indifference is the very message garnered from these events. When citizens are cognizant of the tragedy of the ill, the reputation of the corporate, the plight of government entities, and the agendas of the rich and famous, the simple truths stand on their own merits.

As events spiraled, so too did the community's need to understand a world of science and medicine with which they had formerly shared only a nodding acquaintance. That lack of knowledge is perhaps an important point of the story after all. Ignorance is not bliss when it prevents each of us from understanding the enemies lurking within our midst.

I hope the experience of Beverly Hills ignites a new awareness about our neighborhoods and our role in maintaining wellness standards. Sadly, the pollution problem cannot be confined to one area, economic strata, or level of education. What happened in Beverly Hills is happening in every community. "We assumed the requisite agencies were on top of things," was a mantra adopted by the bulk of city officials who served the community during the years the wells occupied the high school's playfield. Like most other cities and towns across America, Beverly Hills correctly or incorrectly expected the government regulatory agencies to act as environmental guardians. Perhaps that was and remains a common mistake. Underfunded and understaffed, these entities cannot hope to achieve total oversight without help and input from citizens. Until laws are changed and loopholes closed, incidents like that at Beverly Hills will continue to garner untold wealth for lawyers, and more gray hairs for parents of sick children.

We are dependant on cell phones, yet we mistrust their safety. We decry VOCs and vehicle emissions but are unwilling to sacrifice the convenience and freedom of our cars. We buy poison-laced products from countries with no health or environmental standards in order to save money and find ultimately we pay the highest price of all—health and life. Our environmental "stars" fly about, battling pollution in private jets, spewing a noxious chemical trail along the way. The amount of hypocrisy is blatant and egregious. Yet, they are not alone. We the people, after all is said and done, are all about "we the people." We are all partially guilty and our duly elected officials reflect these contradictory attitudes.

There are numerous steps residents can enact to help ensure safety. PTAs can appoint an environmental point person to identify and update their members about potential problems in the schools. They should also act as a liaison between the group and the school board to ensure mitigation measures are carried out. Each school should initiate projects to allow students hands-on activities then track the positive effects of their efforts to clean and "green" their environment.

Residents should insist the city appoint an environmental watchdog to oversee any industries or businesses that may potentially pollute. There should be regular checks that are documented and reported to the community at large twice yearly. Every city or town should include environmental updates on their website. There should also be links to sites that report recalls and product warnings.

Every community can delegate one day a year as Environmental Watchdog Day. On this day residents who have concerns can come before the city council and voice their issues. One point person in the city will address and report on these problems. If there is any suspicion of pollution, air, or water violations, the state agencies should be called to check and monitor the potential offender.

If these suggestions are enlisted in communities, I believe it will cut down greatly on the violations and future health problems that can and do arise daily. I am certain they would have had a great impact on what ultimately happened in Beverly Hills. Reading about the problems Beverly Hills incurred, the effects on its citizenry, and the impacts on the city itself may be a valuable lesson. Many people remain ill today and are unsatisfied with the information they received regarding the safety of the oil well and its emissions. Uncertainty and frustration over the cause of their sickness adds additional stress to their misfortunes. My heart did and always will go out to them with the hope they receive the answers they seek. I suppose until we as a society stop allowing lawmakers to set their priorities on their own war chests in lieu of the public good, we are doomed to remain plagued by our current situation. Despite an all-too-common belief to the contrary, we actually can control our environment. Diligence, caution, and insisting on higher health standards will work wonders without imposing new taxes, eliminating our creature comforts, or lining the coffers of trial lawyers. Only by watching and holding the government and ourselves accountable will we achieve the goals we desire for healthy air, water, soil, and import oversight.

I am certain if we all dedicate ourselves to a cleaner, safer, and informed lifestyle, it will not be long before incidents like Beverly Hills are in the past. My heartfelt wish for all of us is much luck in this endeavor, and most especially, a healthier, safer future for our children and grandchildren. I know it is possible and I am sure we can all look forward to a brighter, "greener" tomorrow.

Alas, but just as is in any typical Hollywood story, one must stay tuned; a sequel may well be in the offing.